iOS Game Development By Example

Learn how to develop an ace game for your
iOS device using Sprite Kit

Samanyu Chopra

[PACKT] open source *
PUBLISHING   community experience distilled

BIRMINGHAM - MUMBAI

iOS Game Development By Example

First published: August 2015

Production reference: 1240815

Published by Packt Publishing Ltd.
Livery Place
35 Livery Street
Birmingham B3 2PB, UK.

ISBN 978-1-78528-469-4

www.packtpub.com

Cover image by Raju Mondal (raju@daphnislabs.com)

Credits

Author
Samanyu Chopra

Reviewers
Chady Kassouf

Joni Mikkola

Jayant Varma

Commissioning Editor
Dipika Gaonkar

Acquisition Editor
Subho Gupta

Content Development Editor
Akashdeep Kundu

Technical Editor
Tanmayee Patil

Copy Editor
Angad Singh

Project Coordinator
Milton Dsouza

Proofreader
Safis Editing

Indexer
Rekha Nair

Production Coordinator
Manu Joseph

Cover Work
Manu Joseph

About the Author

Samanyu Chopra is a developer, entrepreneur, and game developer with a bank of experience in conceptualizing, developing, and producing computer and mobile software. He has been programming since the age of 11. He is proficient in programming languages such as JavaScript, Scala, C#, C++, Swift, and so on. He has a wide range of experience in developing for computers and mobiles. He has worked on a majority of game engines and mobile platforms, and also has a strong proficiency in the Scala programming language.

He is the cofounder and CEO of Daphnis Labs, a mobile app and game development studio. He has experience in managing development, leading the tech jargon, and has published over 150 apps and games for himself and his clients. In his studio, he leads a team of more than 20 members. He is known for executing eccentric projects in the app and game development spaces. He also conducts mobile development workshops at various engineering institutes.

He is ardent about his work, and his colleagues, students, and coworkers think of him as a very dedicated and open-minded person. He is inclined toward investing his time in the research and development of new technologies.

He is an avid traveler and adventurer and a very fun-loving and eccentric personality, as described by the people around him. He has an undying love for travel, tech, and comedy. He is inspired by all the people who have made a stand on their own from scratch. He loves his family and dedicates his life to them.

You can know more about Daphnis Labs at `www.DaphnisLabs.com`. You can write a tweet to him at `@samdonly1` or find him on Facebook for any updates. You can also reach him at `samanyu@DaphnisLabs.com`.

I would like to thank everyone at Packt Publishing who helped in carving this book, including my acquisition editor, Subho Gupta, content development editor, Akashdeep Kundu, technical editor, Tanmayee Patil, and especially the reviewers. Writing this book has been a remarkable experience for me and it wouldn't have been possible without their support and guidance.

I would like to thank all the mentors that I've had over the years. For this book, particularly, I would like to thank my dad, Mukul Chopra, and the iOS lead in our company, Nitin Rajashekhar, for their wisdom and support.

Finally, immense thanks to my family, friends, and team members at Daphnis Labs, who supported me in making games along with helping me teach game development to others. The conceptualization of this book is the result of the motivation and inspiration provided by them.

About the Reviewers

Chady Kassouf is an independent iOS and web development expert. He started programming 23 years ago and hasn't stopped ever since.

7 years ago, he decided to leave his job as a team leader at one of the leading digital agencies to start his own business.

His interests outside of computers include arts, music, and fitness. He can be found online at `http://chady.net/`.

Joni Mikkola is currently working on his next mobile game in Northern Finland. He keeps his game developing stamina up to the mark by training regularly at the gym and eating healthy. While developing games, he often reads books, plays the piano, or bakes buns to keep ideas flowing and his mind focused. He is constantly challenging the status quo, which in turn helps him learn new ways to create things.

He has developed games for over 4 years professionally, mostly for mobile platforms. He targets casual games and focuses on creating simplistic designs. With one game released, he is currently working on his next game, which will be released in late 2015 for the Android and iOS platforms.

Jayant Varma is the founder of OZ Apps (www.oz-apps.com), a consulting, training, and development company that provides IT solutions (specialization in mobile technology). He is an experienced developer with more than 20 years of industry experience in several countries. He is also the author of a number of books on iOS development, including *Learn Lua for iOS Game Development, Apress*. 2012, *Xcode 6 Essentials, Packt Publishing*. 2015, *More iPhone Development with Swift, Apress*. 2015, *More iPhone Development with Objective-C, Apress*. 2015, and *Pro Bash Programming, Apress*. 2015. He has been a university lecturer in Australia, where he currently resides. He loves traveling and Europe is his favorite destination.

www.PacktPub.com

Support files, eBooks, discount offers, and more

For support files and downloads related to your book, please visit www.PacktPub.com.

Did you know that Packt offers eBook versions of every book published, with PDF and ePub files available? You can upgrade to the eBook version at www.PacktPub.com and as a print book customer, you are entitled to a discount on the eBook copy. Get in touch with us at service@packtpub.com for more details.

At www.PacktPub.com, you can also read a collection of free technical articles, sign up for a range of free newsletters and receive exclusive discounts and offers on Packt books and eBooks.

https://www2.packtpub.com/books/subscription/packtlib

Do you need instant solutions to your IT questions? PacktLib is Packt's online digital book library. Here, you can search, access, and read Packt's entire library of books.

Why subscribe?

- Fully searchable across every book published by Packt
- Copy and paste, print, and bookmark content
- On demand and accessible via a web browser

Free access for Packt account holders

If you have an account with Packt at www.PacktPub.com, you can use this to access PacktLib today and view 9 entirely free books. Simply use your login credentials for immediate access.

Table of Contents

Preface

Sprite Kit is a set of tools to develop 2D games for the Apple iOS platform. Sprite Kit provides powerful features for graphics and the animation of images having texture, and so on. It is one of the best available game engines for iOS devices. It is very simple and powerful, with full support provided by Apple, hence it is more reliable and convenient than any third-party game engine available today.

The Integrated Development Environment (IDE), Xcode, provided by Apple for app development can also be used for Sprite Kit game development. Objective-C or Swift, either of the two programming languages can be used for Sprite Kit game development. Sprite Kit is already being used by many developers for iOS game development. There is a good amount of information available that focuses on Sprite Kit set up and development. However, a structured and concise resource discussing about the complete development process and feature set is not currently available. This book explains the basics of Sprite Kit development and allows a beginner to become skilled in Sprite Kit game development using the Swift programming language with its complete set of development features. This book is a complete guide for Sprite Kit and a perfect starting point for those wanting to set sail on the iOS game industry.

What this book covers

Chapter 1, *An Introduction to Sprite Kit*, introduces you to the Sprite Kit game engine, along with its various elements and features. It also helps in setting up a new Xcode project for developing a Sprite Kit game.

Chapter 2, *Scenes in Sprite Kit*, explains an important topic in Sprite Kit, that is, scenes. Along with this, there is a brief about the node tree drawing order.

Chapter 3, *Sprites*, explains sprites and their properties. It also applies some of the properties in the example game.

Chapter 4, *Nodes in Sprite Kit*, discusses about nodes and its subclasses in detail. It also explains the implementation of various node subclasses in the example game.

Chapter 5, *Physics in Sprite Kit*, talks about physics simulation in a Sprite Kit game. It explains the types of physics bodies. Physics capabilities are applied to the example game in this chapter.

Chapter 6, *Animating Sprites, Controls, and SceneKit*, covers animating nodes and adding controls to a Sprite Kit game. These features are added in the example game. It also talks about SceneKit.

Chapter 7, *Particle Effects and Shaders*, discusses about particle effects and shaders, along with their implementation in the example game.

Chapter 8, *Handling Multiple Scenes and Levels*, helps us understand the need for different levels in a game. This chapter also explains how to create multiple scenes.

Chapter 9, *Performance Enhancement and Extras*, discusses in detail how to improve the performance of a Sprite Kit game, along with performance measuring using instruments. It also explains the scoring system, sound, and player running animation in the example game.

Chapter 10, *Revisiting Our Game and More on iOS 9*, discusses the various steps involved in the development of a game, and introduces readers to the Game Center and discusses new features that will be introduced in iOS 9.

What you need for this book

Readers will require Xcode, which is the IDE provided by Apple for developing software, and also the sample game for Mac OS X and iOS devices. An iOS-running device will be helpful to the readers for running the example game that is being developed in the book.

Who this book is for

This book is for beginners who want to start their game development odyssey on the iOS platform. If you are an intermediate or proficient game developer hailing from a different development platform, this book will be the perfect gateway into the Sprite Kit engine. The reader does not need to have any prior knowledge of Sprite Kit, and building games on the iOS platform.

Conventions

In this book, you will find a number of text styles that distinguish between different kinds of information. Here are some examples of these styles and an explanation of their meaning.

Code words in text, database table names, folder names, filenames, file extensions, pathnames, dummy URLs, user input, and Twitter handles are shown as follows: "To make a sprite in a game, we have to make an instance of the SKSpriteNode class."

A block of code is set as follows:

```
init(name: String){
  //it is designated initializer . initialization part


}
convenience init(){
  //Calling the Designated Initializer in same class
  self.init(name: "Hello")
}
```

New terms and **important words** are shown in bold. Words that you see on the screen, for example, in menus or dialog boxes, appear in the text like this: "Untick the **Portrait** checkbox and tick **Landscape Left** under the **Device Orientation** section."

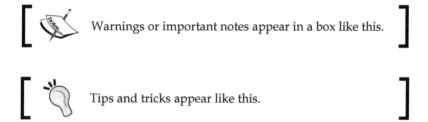

Warnings or important notes appear in a box like this.

Tips and tricks appear like this.

Reader feedback

Feedback from our readers is always welcome. Let us know what you think about this book—what you liked or disliked. Reader feedback is important for us as it helps us develop titles that you will really get the most out of.

To send us general feedback, simply e-mail feedback@packtpub.com, and mention the book's title in the subject of your message.

If there is a topic that you have expertise in and you are interested in either writing or contributing to a book, see our author guide at www.packtpub.com/authors.

Customer support

Now that you are the proud owner of a Packt book, we have a number of things to help you to get the most from your purchase.

Downloading the color images of this book

We also provide you with a PDF file that has color images of the screenshots/ diagrams used in this book. The color images will help you better understand the changes in the output. You can download this file from: `https://www.packtpub.com/sites/default/files/downloads/B04201_4694OS_Graphics.pdf`.

Downloading the example code

You can download the example code files from your account at `http://www.packtpub.com` for all the Packt Publishing books you have purchased. If you purchased this book elsewhere, you can visit `http://www.packtpub.com/support` and register to have the files e-mailed directly to you.

Errata

Although we have taken every care to ensure the accuracy of our content, mistakes do happen. If you find a mistake in one of our books—maybe a mistake in the text or the code—we would be grateful if you could report this to us. By doing so, you can save other readers from frustration and help us improve subsequent versions of this book. If you find any errata, please report them by visiting `http://www.packtpub.com/submit-errata`, selecting your book, clicking on the **Errata Submission Form** link, and entering the details of your errata. Once your errata are verified, your submission will be accepted and the errata will be uploaded to our website or added to any list of existing errata under the Errata section of that title.

To view the previously submitted errata, go to `https://www.packtpub.com/books/content/support` and enter the name of the book in the search field. The required information will appear under the **Errata** section.

Piracy

Piracy of copyrighted material on the Internet is an ongoing problem across all media. At Packt, we take the protection of our copyright and licenses very seriously. If you come across any illegal copies of our works in any form on the Internet, please provide us with the location address or website name immediately so that we can pursue a remedy.

Please contact us at copyright@packtpub.com with a link to the suspected pirated material.

We appreciate your help in protecting our authors and our ability to bring you valuable content.

Questions

If you have a problem with any aspect of this book, you can contact us at questions@packtpub.com, and we will do our best to address the problem.

1
An Introduction to Sprite Kit

In this book we will be discussing about iOS game development using Sprite Kit. We will be taking a fun approach and shall make an actual 2D platform game on the iPhone in the process. We are going to develop a 2D (two dimensional) game; a game which relies on only two coordinates. Some famous 2D games include *Mario*, *Hill Climb Racing*, *Angry Birds*, *Cut the Rope*, and so on.

A 2D game only deals with two dimensions along *x* and *y* axes (left/right and up/down) but not along the *z* axis (forward/backward). So basically, players cannot rotate or move the camera freely in a 3D space to view objects from other angles and perspectives. Although there are exceptions such as 2.5D games; we will be talking about that in later chapters. So, let's not keep things waiting and dive into the book.

What's new in iOS 8?

You might be familiar with Apple's mobile operating system, popularly known as iOS; the latest version of this operating system is iOS 8. This version has a lot of new additions over its predecessor, iOS 7. Some of the additions in this version are the introduction of the Swift programming language, loads of new API's, and most importantly, improvements in Sprite Kit and its peripheral frameworks.

In this book, we will be using the Swift programming language over Objective-C. Although, you can use Sprite Kit with either Objective-C or Swift, Swift offers much easier syntax, and has a simpler learning curve.

Getting to know Swift

Swift is Apple's entirely new multi-paradigm programming language for developing applications on Apple devices. Swift has been in development for 4 years, and was announced in 2014 at the **Worldwide Developer Conference** (**WWDC**). Swift is both, a scripting and programming language; it has the ability to return multiple return values. Swift takes different constructs that are loved from many languages including Objective-C, Rust, Haskell, Ruby, Python, C#, CLU, and more. It has type safety feature that is, to prevent you passing string as int thus minimizing possible errors in your code.

We will be discussing more about Swift, as and when required, in the further topics covered.

Getting to know Sprite Kit

Sprite Kit is a framework from Apple, meant for developing 2D games for iOS devices. It is one of the best ways to make games for iOS devices. It is easy to learn, powerful and fully supported by Apple, which makes it more reliable to use than third-party game development engines.

Sprite Kit was introduced in iOS 7 and allowed easy, fast game development; it has similarities with Cocos2d, which is a popular library for game development. If you are somewhat familiar with Cocos2d, Sprite Kit will be a breeze for you.

Sprite Kit provides various functionalities that are useful for games, such as graphics rendering, animation utilities, sound playback, a particle system, and physics simulation. In Sprite Kit, every node will have a property name and physics body, which can consist of arbitrary shapes such as rectangles, polygons, circles, paths, and so on. Sprite Kit provides a richer particle system, where any aspect can be changed by code during the animation. In Sprite Kit's particle system, you can also add custom actions to the particles created. In addition, Xcode provides built-in support for Sprite Kit so that you can create complex special effects and texture atlases directly in Xcode. This combination of framework and tools makes Sprite Kit a good choice for games and other apps that require similar kinds of animation.

Because Sprite Kit supports a rich rendering infrastructure, and handles all of the low-level work to submit drawing commands to OpenGL, you can focus your efforts on solving higher-level design problems and creating your game functionality.

As Sprite Kit is a native framework of iOS, it provides in-built support for using the particle effects, texture effects, and physics simulations. The performance of Sprite Kit is better than other third-party frameworks/gaming engines, as it is a native framework.

Advantages of Sprite Kit

The main advantage of Sprite Kit is that it's built into iOS. There is no need to download any other third-party libraries or depend on external resources to develop 2D games. Other iOS APIs such as, iAd, In-App purchases, and so on, can be easily used without banking on extra plugins. You don't have to get familiar with any new programming language, the languages supported for Sprite Kit can also be used for app development on iOS. The best thing of all is that it is free, you get all the functionalities of Sprite Kit at no cost. You can run your game on both Mac and iOS without much effort, all you need to do is change its controls.

Elements of Sprite Kit

Now we are going to discuss some elements of Sprite Kit, which are essential for game development. A game made in Sprite Kit consists of many scenes which are made of nodes, and the functioning of a node in a scene is determined by actions.

Scenes

A level or environment in a game is termed as a scene. We make scenes as per our requirement, such as menus, levels, and so on. So, there are different scenes for different levels and also for different menus in a game. It's like a canvas where you position your elements.

A scene in Sprite Kit is represented by an SKScene object. A scene holds sprites and other contents to be rendered. To switch scenes, we can use the SKTransition class.

Nodes

Nodes are fundamental building blocks for all content in a scene. The SKScene class is a descendant of the SKNode class, so a scene is a root node. The SKNode class does not draw anything on scene by itself; we can think of it as a base class for other node classes. There are node subclasses as follows:

- SKSpriteNode: This can be used for drawing textured sprites, playing video content, and more
- SK3DNode: This can be used for rendering a Scene Kit scene as a 2D textured image
- SKVideoNode: This can be used for playing video content
- SKLabelNode: This can be used for rendering a text string

- `SKShapeNode`: This can be used for rendering shape, based on a core graphics path
- `SKEmitterNode`: This can be used for creating and rendering particles
- `SKCropNode`: This can be used for cropping child nodes using a mask
- `SKEffectNode`: This can be used for applying a core image filter to its child node
- `SKLightNode`: This can be used for applying lighting and shadows to a scene
- `SKFieldNode`: This can be used for applying physics effects to a specific portion of the scene

Actions

An action tells a node what to do and allows you to perform different things, such as:

- Moving nodes in any direction
- Making any node follow a path
- Rotating nodes
- Scaling of nodes
- Showing or hiding a node
- Changing the content of a sprite node
- Playing sound
- Removing nodes from a scene
- Performing action on a child's node, and so on

To create a run action, first, create the action using the particular action class, configure the properties for the created action, and call a run action by passing action object as a parameter. When the scene processes the node, the actions of that particular node will be executed.

Features of Sprite Kit

Sprite Kit provides many features to facilitate the development of a game. These features can be used for enhancing the experience as well as performance of the game. Let's discuss them in brief.

Particle editor

This feature was introduced in iOS 7. Particle editor is used to add special effects in a game, like adding a mist effect in a game scene. Here, we can customize many things, such as:

- The number of particles
- Limit of particles allowed
- The color of particles
- The size of a particle
- The life of a particle
- The location of a particle in a scene, and so on

Texture atlas generator

Texture atlas generator combines all image files into one or more large images, in order to improve performance. We will discuss this in detail in the later chapters. It is recommended to use a lesser number of images to reduce draw calls (number of images rendering on a scene).

Shaders

Shaders were introduced in iOS 8. They are used to produce a variety of special effects; they calculate rendering effects on graphic hardware with a high degree of flexibility, for example, we have seen ripple effects in many apps/games. Wherever a user touches the screen, a ripple effect will be produced.

In Sprite Kit, shaders are represented by the SKShaderNode class object.

Lighting and shadows

Lighting and shadows were introduced in iOS 8. These effects are produced using the SKLightNode class object. The SKLightNode object can:

- Spread a lighting effect at any desirable position on the scene
- Add lighting in any sprite
- Support colors and shadows

It's just a type SKNode, so we can apply any property that we apply to any SKNode.

Physics

Simulating physics in Sprite Kit can be achieved by adding physics bodies to the scenes. A physics engine has the sole purpose of moving objects around in a simulated world. The physics bodies take the properties of objects, such as mass, shape material, current trajectory, and so on, and calculate a new position for all those objects.

Every object on the Sprite Kit game scene will have a physics body. A physics body object is connected to a node on the node tree of a particular scene. The scene will simulate the effect of forces and collisions on those particular physics bodies that are connected to the node tree, whenever the scene computes a new frame of animation. We can apply a particular physics property on those nodes using their particular physics properties such as gravity, mass, force, friction, and so on.

The game loop

Following is a frame life cycle diagram:

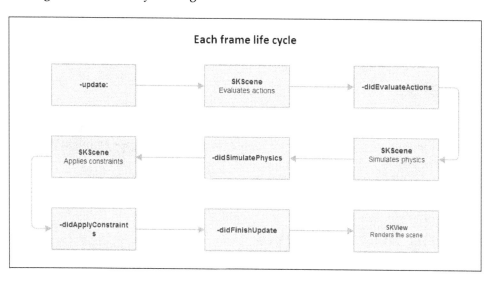

At the start, the update function is called to where we set up the logic of the game. After that, the scene evaluates the actions. After the actions are evaluated, we get a callback. After that, we set up physics, if any. When the physics simulation is finished, we get another call with didSimulatePhysics. Then, we apply constraint and get another callback, didApplyConstraints. The last callback method is didFinishUpdate; we get it just before frame is completed and view is ready to render. Finally SKView renders the scene; the frame is complete and it continues 60 times per second.

Setting up a project

We have discussed many things about Sprite Kit, now it's time to see a project in action and gain some practical knowledge.

The Hello World project

We'll need to create a new project to build Hello World. An Xcode project organizes everything your app needs into one convenient place. Let's begin by creating a brand new game project in Xcode by carrying out either of the first two points, and then continuing as shown in the list:

1. Click on **Create a new Xcode project** on the welcome screen:

2. Instead, you can also select **File | New | Project...** from the file menu:

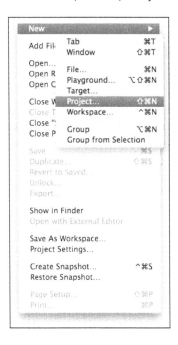

3. Select **Game** from the new project selection window:

4. The next window asks you to customize options for your project. Fill out the fields as shown in the following screenshot:

- ○ **Product Name**: It is the name of the game
- ○ **Organization Name**: If you are an individual, then your name, or the name of the organization
- ○ **Organization Identifier**: A unique identifier of your organization
- ○ **Bundle Identifier**: It is a default ID generated automatically using organization identifier and product name.
- ○ **Language**: The programming language you are using, that is, Objective-C or Swift
- ○ **Game Technology**: The game framework being used, like Scene Kit, Sprite Kit, Metal, and so on
- ○ **Devices**: The devices you want your game to run on; iPad, iPhone, or both
- ○ These fields can be anything you want

5. Press **Next** and Xcode will ask where to save your new project. Choose a directory and then click on **Create**.

6. After saving, it should open Xcode to your brand new `Hello World` project, specifically to the project properties screen. On this screen, unselect the **Portrait** option under **Device Orientation**. This file will be automatically saved, so you won't have to do anything further:

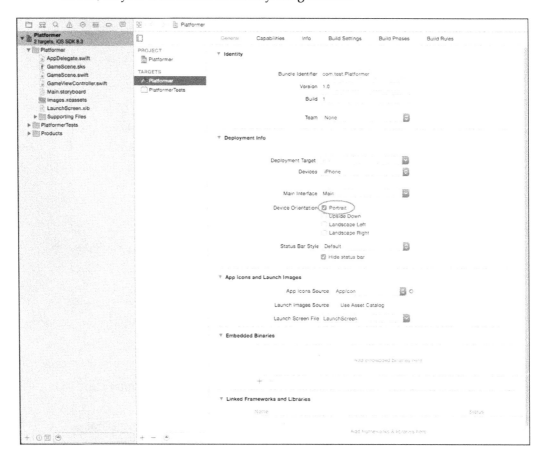

Result

Run the default game project by pressing ⌘ + R on your keyboard, or by clicking on the little play button in the top left corner. If a simulator isn't present, Xcode will download one for you before launching the app. The result will look as follows:

Summary

We also learned how to create a Sprite Kit project and run `Hello World` in it.

In the next chapter, we will be diving deeply into scenes, and also into adding scenes to our *Platformer* game.

2
Scenes in Sprite Kit

The *Hello World* game, made in the previous chapter. was the first step to Sprite Kit. We also made acquaintance with the Swift programming language, which we are going to use for iOS game development using Sprite Kit.

In this chapter, we will dive deep into various fundamentals of the Sprite Kit project and also discuss in depth about scenes in a game. We are further going to continue the development of the game, *Platformer*, and use it as a tool to learn Sprite Kit. We will be learning about different auto generated files in an Xcode project and about their importance. Only then will we be able to understand what scenes are, and their importance in game development. Further we will also learn how nodes play an important part in Sprite Kit and help us to improve optimization and control of our game. In this chapter, we will also learn how to add more than one scene in our game and successfully transit from one scene to another along with animating various transition effects.

We will be learning all of this and testing our progress with development of the game *Platformer*, so that by the end of the book, you are able make your own 2D game from scratch. Let's get going!

Device orientation in Sprite Kit

There are two types of modes, namely portrait and landscape; you can select the desired orientation for your game while setting up your project. Any time during the development of your game, you can change the orientation under the properties section of your Sprite Kit project. There are four types of orientations available:

- Portrait
- Upside Down
- Landscape Left
- Landscape Right

You can select any of the orientations depending on your game. If you want to make your game scene in portrait mode, you can select either **Portrait** or **Upside Down** options. If want to make your game in landscape mode, you can select the **Landscape Left** or **Landscape Right** option. If you want to make your game in both portrait and landscape, then you can select both the options too. Caution, if you want to make your game in both portrait and landscape mode, make sure that you have to handle the positions of sprites in your game during runtime.

Orientation in our project

As we are making a *Platformer* game, it's better to opt for landscape mode. Although you can select both **Landscape Left** and **Landscape Right**, it is better to opt for one orientation for easier programming. Following are the steps to do the same:

1. Launch the `Platformer` project that we made in the last chapter, either by double-clicking `Platformer.xcodeproj` from the directory of project, or from your Xcode.

2. Click on the **Project Navigator** and then click **Platformer**, which is just under it, on the left panel.

3. Untick the **Portrait** checkbox and tick **Landscape Left** under the **Device Orientation** section:

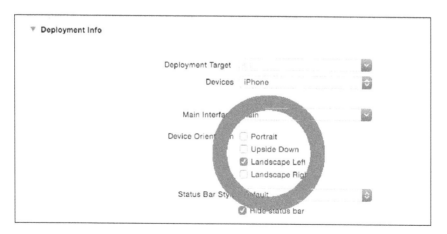

Revisiting project elements

Now we are going to discuss about some auto-generated files in your Sprite Kit project. They can be found on the left panel in your Xcode.

AppDelegate.swift

This file is an entry point file to our game. Its existence is crucial when the game goes from an active state to inactive state (or background state), in simple terms, when there are some sorts of temporary interruptions (such as incoming phone calls or SMS messages), or when the user force quits the application. The essence of this file in a project comes when you have to perform any specific task between the transition of active and inactive states, such as saving game data when the game is moving into a background state due to a phone call.

GameScene.sks

This file is a static archive of your scene's content. This file presents a view in your editor, it is used to save static content of a game such as spawning the position of a player, level ending position, and so on. The main essence and importance of this file is that it has worked towards helping you to separate the dynamic and static part of a game. Now a developer does not need to write extra lines of code for specifying trivial elements of a game such as spawning position, and so on.

GameScene.swift

This file contains the `GameScene` class which is a type of `SKScene`. An `SKScene` class object is used to make a scene in a game. When we developed the "Hello World" sample game in the previous chapter, the logic part was present inside this file.

GameViewController.swift

When a game starts, a default view is added to the game, which is controlled by the game view controller. If the user wants to add scenes to the game, then it is added on top of the view.

Main.storyboard

This is responsible for displaying content on the screen. A storyboard with a view controller whose view is set to `SKView` is created, the scene then displays the content of the Sprite Kit game. You can create additional view controllers and storyboards along with applying transition between them.

LaunchScreen.xib

New projects are created with this launch screen file. The Launch Screen uses size classes to adapt to different screen sizes and orientations.

Adjusting the project

We are going to make some adjustments in the already-created project called `Platformer`. Please follow the steps listed, in order to customize the project according to our needs:

1. Delete the `GameScene.swift` and `GameScene.sks` files present in your project. We will be recreating these files as per our need. Don't worry about the error, we are going to fix it in the next step. `GameScene.swift` is the default scene given by Xcode; we are deleting the default ones as we are going to create the menu Scene before the game scene. Take a look at the next screenshot:

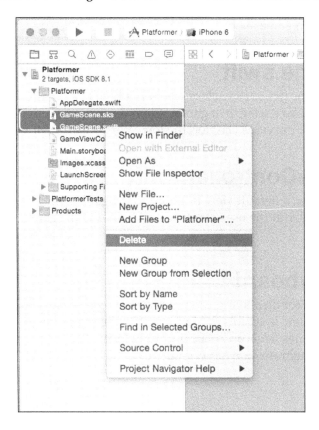

2. Open `GameViewController.swift` and delete the code, as shown in the following screenshot:

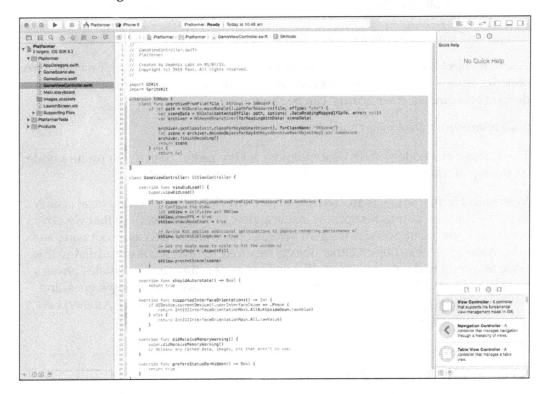

3. Delete the **Spaceship** image from `Images.xcassets`. Spaceship images are not required in this project.

Now you will not see an error in your Xcode, and if you run `Platformer`, you will see nothing. Well, that is not what we desire. Now, before getting your feet wet in code, we need to know what we have done (almost nothing but deleting) so far:

- **Extension SKNode**: This extension is inserted by Sprite Kit presuming that every game must have an initial scene, creating a GameScene.sks file. We do not need this initial scene at the start of our *Platformer* game, as we will create our own menu screen on start.

- **If statement within viewDidLoad**: As `GameScene.sks` file created by extension `SKNode` is used in this statement.

Now we are going to create our own custom scene for this game, but before that, let's now see what a scene really is.

What is a scene?

A scene is basically a collection of different elements such as sprites, sounds, and so on, in a logical way. Suppose we want to make a menu, we'll have to put some buttons, background, and sounds in a manner that is positioned according to our needs.

A Scene object is a collection of nodes, but a scene itself acts as a node. Imagine a tree of nodes having scene objects as its root. As all nodes in the scene are positioned in defined coordinates, their linkage can be shown as:

Node (Content) → *Descendant Node*

This linkage of a node with its descendant(s) is very useful. Say, if you rotate a node on the top of the tree, all the nodes will be subsequently rotated.

In technical terms, Scene is an SKScene object, which holds an SKNode object (such as SKSpriteNode objects for sprites) inside a view (SKView object), so that we can render and use them. Scene is itself an SKNode object, which acts as a root node and attaches in an SKView object. Other objects required for that scene are added to this node as a child node. A scene runs different kinds of actions and simulates physics (if required), and then renders the node tree. A game consists of many scenes, and we can make as many scenes required by sub-classing SKScene class. An SKView object is required to display a scene.

Coordinate system

Everything in a game built in Sprite Kit is related to nodes, and it follows a node tree structure where a scene is a root node and other nodes are child nodes of it. When we put a node in the node tree, it uses its position property to place it within the coordinate system provided by its parent.

As a scene is also a node, it is placed inside the view provided by the SKView object. The code part which we deleted in viewDidLoad, GameScene, was added as a child in the SKView object. A scene uses its parent SKView object coordination system to render itself and the content within it. The coordinate system is the same as we learned in basic mathematics.

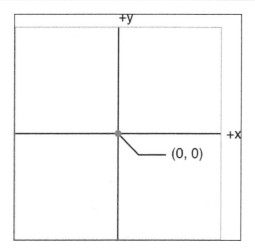

As the preceding diagram shows, if we move right from **(0,0)**, then **x** will be positive, and negative if we move left from **(0,0)**. If we move up from **(0,0)**, then **y** will be positive, and negative if we move down from **(0,0)**. Coordinate values are measured in points and when the scene is rendered, it will be converted to pixels.

All the nodes in Sprite Kit will not draw the content. For example, SKSpriteNode is used to draw sprites in a game, but SKNode class does not draw anything as SKNode is a fundamental building block for most Sprite Kit content.

Creating a scene

When we create a scene, we can define many of its properties such as size, origin, and so on. as we require in our game. A scene size defines the visible area in the **SKView** object. Of course, we can put nodes outside this area, but they will be totally ignored by the renderer.

However, if we try to change the position property of a scene, it will be ignored by Sprite Kit because a scene is a root node in a node tree, its default value is CGPointZero. But we can move scene origin by the anchorPoint property. Default value for anchorPoint is (0.5,0.5), which indicates the center point of the screen. By reassigning a new anchorPoint property, we can change the coordinate system for its child. For example, if we set anchorPoint to (0,0), the child node of the scene will start from the bottom left of the scene.

If we make the anchorPoint (0.5, 0.5) or the middle of the screen, the child node of the scene will start from the middle of the screen. It totally depends on us and what anchorPoint we choose as per our requirement.

Creating a node tree

A node tree for a scene is created as a parent child relation. As a scene acts similar to a root node, another node acts as a child to it. Following are some common methods used to make a node tree:

- `addChild`: It adds a node to the end of the receiver's list of child nodes
- `insertChild:atIndex`: It inserts a child at a specific position in the receiver's list of child nodes

If you want to remove a node from a node tree, you can use the following method:

- `removeFromParent`: It removes the receiving node from its parent

Drawing order for a node tree

When a node tree renders, all its children also render. First, the parent is rendered, and then, its children, in the order they are added to parent. If you have many nodes to render in a scene, it is a difficult task to maintain them in order. For this, Sprite Kit provides a solution using the z position. You can set nodes to the z position by using the `zPosition` property.

When you take the z position into account, the node tree will be rendered as follows:

- First of all, each node's global z position is calculated
- Then, nodes are drawn in order from smallest z value to largest z value
- If two nodes share the same z value, ancestors are rendered first, and siblings are rendered in child order

As you've just seen, Sprite Kit uses a deterministic rendering order, based on the height nodes and their positions in the node tree. But, because the rendering order is so deterministic, Sprite Kit may be unable to apply some rendering optimizations that it might otherwise apply. For example, it might be better if Sprite Kit could gather all of the nodes that share the same texture and drawing mode and draw them with a single drawing pass. To enable these sorts of optimizations, you have to set the view's `ignoresSiblingOrder` property to `true`.

When you ignore sibling order, Sprite Kit uses the graphics hardware to render the nodes so that they appear in z-axis order. It sorts nodes into a drawing order that reduces the number of draw calls needed to render the scene. But with this optimized drawing order, you cannot predict the rendering order for nodes that share the same z-axis index. The rendering order may change each time a new frame is rendered. In many cases, the drawing order of these nodes is not important. For example, if the nodes are at the same height but do not overlap on screen, they can be drawn in any order.

So, we can use node tree-based rendering or depth-based rendering, just by setting the `ignoresSiblingOrder` property to `false` or `true`. If we set it to true, we can set z position, but if set to false, we have to be careful about sequence when adding child node to parent node.

Following is a depiction of node-based rendering (parent child rendering):

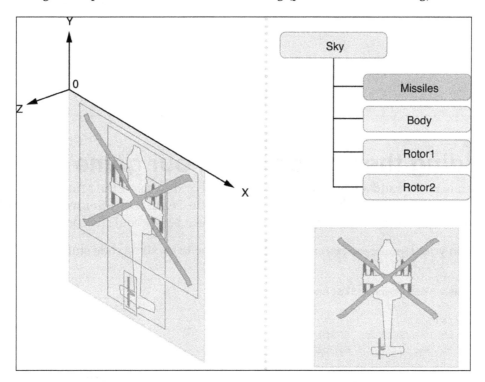

Next is a depiction of depth-based rendering (z position-based rendering):

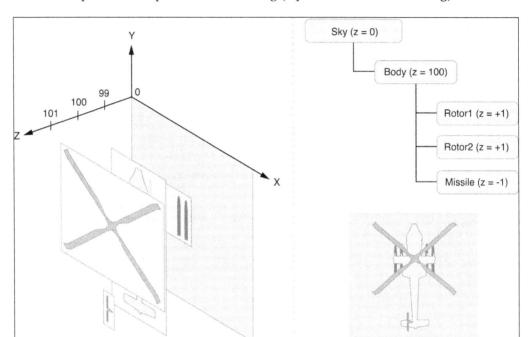

Adding the first scene in our game

Now it is time to add a menu scene to our game. For this, select the Platformer folder and right-click on this folder, select **New File**. Select **iOS | Source | Swift File** and then **Next**. Inside **Save As**, give it the name MenuScene, and click on **Create**.

Click on your MenuScene.swift file. Now it's time to do some code stuff:

```
import SpriteKit
class MenuScene: SKScene
{
  //#1
  let PlayButton: SKSpriteNode
  let Background: SKSpriteNode
  //#2
  init(size:CGSize, playbutton:String, background:String)
  {
    PlayButton = SKSpriteNode(imageNamed: playbutton)
    Background = SKSpriteNode(imageNamed: background)
    super.init(size:size)
  }
  //#3
```

```
required init?(coder aDecoder: NSCoder)
{
    fatalError("init(coder:) has not been implemented")
}
//#4
override func didMoveToView(view: SKView)
{
    addChildToScene();

}
//#5
func addChildToScene()
{
    PlayButton.zPosition = 1
    Background.zPosition = 0
    Background.size = CGSize(width:self.size.width,
    height:self.size.height)
    addChild(PlayButton)
    addChild(Background)
}
//#6
override func update(currentTime: NSTimeInterval) {

}
}
```

In the preceding code, we created a class `MenuScene` type of `SKScene`. `SKScene` is a class used to create scene. Let's look out for some terminology used in this code:

- In the `#1` code block (refer to the preceding code), we define two `SKSpriteNode` references. One for play button and the other for background. The `let` keyword denotes that once we assign a value to this reference, we can't change it. If you want to change that, you should use the `var` keyword instead of `let`.

- In the `#2` code block (refer to the preceding code), we define an initializer for this class. The initializer is used to create an instance of a particular type. Inside this, we initialize `PlayButton` and `Background`. We give background a full screen size by setting its `size` property. In the end, we call parent class `init` by `super.init`.

- In the `#3` code block (refer to the preceding code), we remove errors at compile time. The required keyword denotes that every subclass of that class must implement that initializer.

- In the `#4` code block (refer to the preceding code), we override its parent class method. The `didMoveToView` is called immediately after a scene is presented by a view. We have called our custom method `addChildToScene` here.

- In the #5 code block (refer to the preceding code), we define our addChildToScene method. Inside this we did nothing but give z position to PlayButton and defined size for Background. Remember, we can use z depth to control which layer will render above what. If you have z depth set to minimum, it will render first, and then to maximum. It means that the lower the z depth, the lower it will be in a scene. That's why we put the Background z depth lower than PlayButton, so that PlayButton could render above Background. After that, we added PlayButton and Background to scene.

- In the #6 code block (refer to the preceding code), we just override the update method. The code for this method will be updated later.

Whoa! We have created our first scene. Now it's time to see what we have done. But before that, we have to add this scene to the view, so that we can make it visible and live. Open your GameViewController class and paste the code inside viewDidLoad under super.viewDidLoad():

```
let menuscene = MenuScene(size: view.bounds.size, playbutton:
"Play", background: "BG")
let skview = view as SKView
skview.showsFPS = true
skview.showsNodeCount = true
skview.ignoresSiblingOrder = true
menuscene.scaleMode = .ResizeFill
menuscene.anchorPoint = CGPoint(x: 0.5, y: 0.5)
skview.presentScene(menuscene)
```

In this code, we created the menuscene instance and added it to the view. Play and BG are the names of the PNG sprite, which we will add later. We have typecast view as SKView and set some of its properties. If we want to see frame per second rate, we set showFPS to true. Same goes for the counting node. If we set ignoresSiblingOrder property to false, then it means that the nodes that are sharing the same z depth will be rendered in parent to child preference.

This implies that the parent will render first and then its child. If we set it true, then it means that all the nodes with the same z depth will render at the same time, and not by some parent child preference. So to maximize the optimization, we will just set this value to true; in simple terms, it's better to set this to true if you want faster results.

.scaleMode is used to fill the scene inside a view. ResizeFill means that it will resize itself to fill the whole view.

Now, for the `anchorPoint`. It decides what would be a child's coordinate system according to parent position. If we set it to `.5`, `.5`, that means that the nodes that will be added to these scenes, will have their coordinate system starting from the middle of the screen. You can choose whatever you are comfortable with.

In the last line, we just added `menuscene` to the view so that it could render.

Now, it's time to add some images to the project. The first question that comes to mind is, "How one can maintain the quality of an image on various screen sizes?"

To optimize the quality of an image on large screen devices, we add the same image in two different sizes, 1x—the original image—and 2x—double the size of the original image, for better display quality on larger devices. iOS will automatically select the appropriate image size.

Also, you can go for a 3x image size, for even larger devices.

Two sets of image sizes are sufficient to cover most commonly used screen sizes.

Following are the steps to add images in the project:

1. Click on `Images.xcassets` | select **New Image Set**:

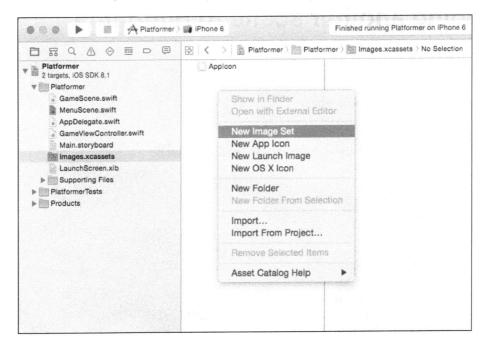

2. After that, Name it BG, and drag and drop your background images according to size. As shown in the next image:

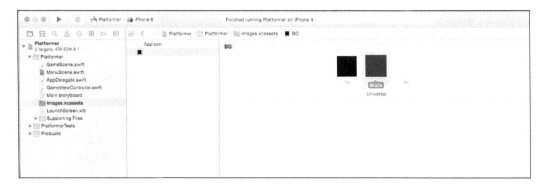

3. Repeat the process for the set of play images.

4. Run it and see. You will see your background in full screen, with a **Play** button in the middle of the screen. We can also control the **Play** button size, as we did for Background.

Congratulations, you made your first scene. Now it's time to make another scene, that is the GameScene, and also transition between MenuScene and Gamescene.

Adding another scene to our game

Create the GameScene file as we did for MenuScene:

```swift
import SpriteKit

class GameScene: SKScene
{

  let backgroundNode = SKSpriteNode(imageNamed: "BG")


  override func didMoveToView(view: SKView) {
  addBackGround()
}

  func addBackGround()
  {
    backgroundNode.zPosition = 0
    backgroundNode.size = CGSize(width:self.size.width,
    height:self.size.height)
```

```
        addChild(backgroundNode)
    }

    override func update(currentTime: NSTimeInterval) {

    }

}
```

The code is self-explanatory, we added only a background to the GameScene, the same as what we did for the MenuScene.

A transition from one scene to another

A transition is used to perform animation; while shifting from one scene to another, an object called SKTransition is used to perform this action. As we know, scenes are the basic building blocks of games. Transiting from one scene to another is often necessary in a game at various instances such as:

- A loading scene, which is shown in a game while other objects are being loaded
- A main menu scene, in which different options are shown to the user
- A level selection menu scene, to select different levels available
- A game play scene, which contains the main elements of the game
- A game over scene, to represent ending of the game, and so on

When you present a new scene in a view that is already presenting a scene, you have the option of using a transition to animate the change from the old scene into the new scene. Using a transition provides continuity, so that the scene change is not abrupt and doesn't disturb the UI of the game.

When the transition occurs, the scene property is immediately updated to point to the new scene. Then, the animation occurs. Finally, the strong reference to the old scene is removed. If you need to keep the scene around after the transition occurs, your game has to keep its own strong reference to the old scene.

Downloading the example code

You can download the example code files from your account at http://www.packtpub.com for all the Packt Publishing books you have purchased. If you purchased this book elsewhere, you can visit http://www.packtpub.com/support and register to have the files e-mailed directly to you.

Setting animation play during transition

Generally, when a transition occurs between two scenes, both the scenes are paused. This implies that if any animation is being played in any one of the two scenes, it will be paused until the transition has been completed. Sometimes, it is required to complete the animation effect of one scene. The pausesIncomingScene and pausesOutgoingScene properties on the transition object define which animations are played during the transition.

Creating transition objects

Transitions are used by making SKTransition an object; some of the methods to do that are as follows:

- class func crossFadeWithDuration(_ sec: NSTimeInterval) -> SKTransition: This creates a cross fade transition; it takes the duration of transition as its parameter and returns an SKTransition object.

- class func doorsCloseHorizontalWithDuration(_ sec: NSTimeInterval) -> SKTransition: This creates a transition where the new scene appears as a pair of closing horizontal doors; it also takes the duration of transition as its parameter and returns an SKTransition object.

- class func doorsCloseVerticalWithDuration(sec: NSTimeInterval) -> SKTransition: This creates a transition where the new scene appears as a pair of closing vertical doors. It also takes the duration of transition as its parameter and returns an SKTransition object.

- class func doorsOpenHorizontalWithDuration(_ sec: NSTimeInterval) -> SKTransition: This creates a transition where the new scene appears as a pair of opening horizontal doors. It also takes the duration of transition as its parameter and returns an SKTransition object.

- class func doorsOpenVerticalWithDuration(_ sec: NSTimeInterval) -> SKTransition: This creates a transition where the new scene appears as a pair of opening vertical doors. It also takes the duration of transition as its parameter and returns an SKTransition object.

- class func doorwayWithDuration(_ sec: NSTimeInterval) -> SKTransition: This creates a transition where the previous scene disappears as a pair of opening doors. The new scene starts in the background and moves closer as the doors open. It also takes the duration of transition as its parameter and returns an SKTransition object.

- `class func fadeWithColor(_ color: UIColor, duration sec: NSTimeInterval) -> SKTransition`: This creates a transition that first fades to a constant color, and then fades to the new scene. It takes the fade color and the duration of transition as parameters, and returns the `SKTransition` as object.

- `class func fadeWithDuration(_ sec: NSTimeInterval) -> SKTransition`: This creates a transition that first fades to black and then fades to the new scene. It takes the duration of transition as its parameter and returns an `SKTransition` object.

- `class func flipHorizontalWithDuration(_ sec: NSTimeInterval) -> SKTransition`: This creates a transition where the two scenes are flipped across a horizontal line running through the center of the view. It takes the duration of transition as its parameter and returns an `SKTransition` object.

- `class func flipVerticalWithDuration(_ sec: NSTimeInterval) -> SKTransition`: This creates a transition where the two scenes are flipped across a vertical line running through the center of the view. It takes the duration of transition as its parameter and returns an `SKTransition` object.

- `class func moveInWithDirection(_ direction: SKTransitionDirection, duration sec: NSTimeInterval) -> SKTransition`: This creates a transition where the new scene moves on top of the old scene. It takes the direction of the move and the duration as its parameters, and returns an SKTransition object.

- `class func pushWithDirection(_ direction: SKTransitionDirection, duration sec: NSTimeInterval) -> SKTransition`: This creates a transition where the new scene moves in, pushing the old scene out of the view. It takes the direction of the push and the duration of transition as its parameters, and returns an SKTransition object.

- `class func revealWithDirection(_ direction: SKTransitionDirection, duration sec: NSTimeInterval) -> SKTransition`: This creates a transition where the old scene moves out of the view, revealing the new scene underneath it. It takes the direction of the reveal and the duration of transition as its parameters, and returns an `SKTransition` object.

Adding transition in our game

Now, open `MenuScene`. First, define the `GameScene` reference inside the `MenuScene` class, before the init code block:

```
var gameScene : GameScene?
Add the following code below update function
override func touchesBegan(touches: NSSet, withEvent event: UIEvent)
{
  for touch: AnyObject in touches
  {
    let location = touch.locationInNode(self)
    let node = self.nodeAtPoint(location)
    if node.name == PlayButton.name
    {
      goToGameScene()
    }
  }
}


  func goToGameScene(){
  let transitionEffect =
  SKTransition.flipHorizontalWithDuration(1.0)
  gameScene = GameScene(size: self.size)
  gameScene!.anchorPoint = CGPoint(x: 0.5, y: 0.5)
  self.view?.presentScene(gameScene , transition:transitionEffect)

  }
```

Inside `didMoveToView`, place the following line just under `addChildToScene`:

```
PlayButton.name = "PLAY"
```

If you run it now, you will see our menu scene with a play button and a background; if you click outside the play button, nothing will happen. When you click on the play button, you will see a smooth transition to the game scene.

In the preceding code, `var` is a keyword that means it can change its value. But what is this `?` symbol doing after `GameScene`?

The `?` symbol means that the reference is optional. It means it can either have a value, or it can be nil.

That's why we don't need to initialize it in the init code block.

In `PlayButton.name = "PLAY"` we are just giving the `SKSpriteNode` object a name, so that when we touch this sprite, we can verify it by name.

`touchesBegan`, is an override method which is used to identify when a touch event is just beginning. In this method, we are getting a node at the touch position and checking if the desired node is there. If the play `SKSpriteNode` is there, it will be identified by its name and will call the `goToGameScene` method.

In `goToGameScene` method, we just added `GameScene` to the view with some transition effect. Transitions are an `SKTransition` class instance. Here, we used the `flipHorizontalWithDuration` transition effect.

You can also tweak and play with other transitions available.

In `gameScene!.anchorPoint = CGPoint(x: 0.5, y: 0.5)`, we have put an exclamation mark after `GameScene`. As we know that `GameScene` is optional, we have to tell the compiler that we know it has a value, and that we are forcing the it to unwrap its value. The `!` symbol is used for force unwrapping optional values.

Summary

In this chapter, we learned about device orientation and about the different auto generated files in a Sprite Kit project. Also, we studied scenes and saw how to create them in a Sprite Kit project. Furthermore, we discussed about transitions between scenes and their types.

In the next chapter, we will learn about sprites and texture atlases. Our *Platformer* game will become much more exciting and interesting to play, as we move further.

3
Sprites

In the previous chapter, we set up our first scene, learned about the rendering of nodes in a scene, added multiple scenes in a project, and learned about doing transitions from one scene to another.

In this chapter, we will learn about sprites. A sprite is a two-dimensional image, integrated into scene. A collection of sprites is called **sprite sheet**. Here we will learn about how to add sprites in a game, positioning a sprite, texture atlases, and how to transform a sprite in our game.

In Sprite Kit, a game is based on the node tree hierarchy. Scene acts as a root node and other nodes added to it are child nodes. Once all nodes are rendered into scene, we get the view. Sprites are also added to a game as a node; Sprite Kit provide us SKSpriteNode class for this purpose. In the previous chapter, we added background sprite and play button sprite by making the SKSpriteNode reference and adding it to the respective scenes. Now we will discover more about what Sprite Kit provided us in the SKSpriteNode class, and what else we can do with it.

SKSpriteNode

The SKSpriteNode class is a root node class which is used to draw texture images with many customizations; it is inherited from the SKNode class. We can simply draw an image, or we can add some effects, such as custom shader or shadows to it. For this, we have to first know about the SKSpriteNode class and the functionality it offers.

Initializing a sprite

To make a sprite in a game, we have to make an instance of the SKSpriteNode class. Sprite Kit provides us with many ways to initialize an instance of the SKSpriteNode class. Some of them are as follows:

```
init(name: String){
   //it is designated initializer . initialization part

}
convenience init(){
   //Calling the Designated Initializer in same class
   self.init(name: "Hello")
}
```

In Swift, one has to initialize a class by making an object of structure. There are two initializers provided for this purpose, that is, designated initializers and convenience initializers.

Designated initializers perform actual initialization for class properties. Now the question arises, "why convenience initializers are required?" During programming, sometimes, convenience initializers are very useful as they require less input parameters, and hand over actual initialization to designated initializers.

Some examples of initializers in Swift are as follows:

- convenience init(color color:UIColor!, size size: CGSize): This is used to initialize a colored sprite. If you want to make a sprite without using any texture and only by color, you can use this. It takes color and size as a parameter and returns a newly initialized sprite object.

- convenience init(imageNamed name: String): This initializer assigns texture to sprites. A sprite will be assigned texture from image name, which initializes the color of a sprite to white.

- convenience init(texture texture: SKTexture!): This initializer takes an existing texture sprite and returns a newly initialized sprite. The size of the sprite is set to the dimensions of the texture, and the color of the sprite is set to white (1.0, 1.0, 1.0).

- init(texture texture: SKTexture!,color color: UIColor!,size size: CGSize): As explained earlier, this initializer requires convenience initializers as its parameter, so this is a designated initializer. Now, our *Platformer* game sprite will be initialized to the desired texture, color, and size. It returns a newly initialized sprite.

- `convenience init(texture texture: SKTexture!,size size: CGSize)`: This takes texture and size as parameters and returns a newly initialized sprite.

- `convenience init(imageNamed name: String, normalMapped generateNormalMap: Bool)`: This takes an image name and a Boolean value as a parameter and returns a newly initialized object.

- `convenience init(texture texture: SKTexture!,normalMap normalMap: SKTexture?)`: This takes two textures as parameters, one for sprite drawing and another for adding lighting behavior to the sprite. It returns a newly initialized sprite.

After learning about initialization of `SKSpriteNode`, now it is time to get ourselves familiar with some physical properties of `SKSpriteNode`, such as `size`, `anchorPoint`, and so on.

The properties of SKSpriteNode

Let us discuss the properties of `SKSpriteNode` in the following sections.

Physical

Let us look at some physical properties of `SKSpriteNode`:

- `size`: This property determines the size of a sprite in points. In our `GameScene` and `MenuScene` classes, we use this property in the background sprite to cover the screen.

- `AnchorPoint`: An anchor point is a point of co-ordinate related to sprite. Say, for example, co-ordinates for each corner of a sprite are `(0,0)`, `(1,0)`, `(0,1)`, and `(1,1)` representing corners bottom left, bottom right, top left, and top right respectively. These points of reference can be assigned as anchor points to draw a sprite on screen in respect. An assigned anchor point will position a sprite on screen, accordingly.

  For example, assume that our anchor point for a sprite is `(0,0)`. If we position this sprite on screen, it will place itself from co-ordinate `(0,0)`, that is, bottom left. To position a sprite from the centre, we need to assign the anchor point co-ordinate `(0.5, 0.5)`.

But to add another node to this sprite, co-ordinate (0,0) of that node will be on the sprite's anchor point. What happens when we add scene to the view is that, co-ordinate (0,0) of scene, becomes the default anchor point.

Physical properties of a sprite were well discussed under `size` and `anchorPoint`. Now it is time to discuss some properties which are related to texture in a sprite.

Texture

It is an optional property in the `SKSpriteNode` class; that means it can be nil or will have texture. If it is nil, then the sprite will be drawn by using its `color` property in a rectangular shape, otherwise the sprite will be drawn using this texture.

centerRect

This property is a very useful tool for creating rectangular buttons or any other fixed size elements in scene. When you use the `centerRect` property, you are actually controlling the scaling factor of texture for a rectangular portion specified by coordinates.

By default, the rectangle covers the whole texture; that's why entire texture is stretched. But if this rectangle covers only a portion of the texture, then the texture could be visualized in a 3 * 3 grid, accounting this rectangle in the middle of the grid and drawing a line from its every edge on each side.

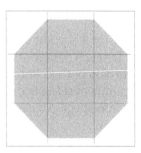

Original image

If we try to stretch the texture in both directions, then it will follow the rules given as follows:

- The middle portion of the grid will stretch on each side, horizontally and vertically
- All 4 corner portions of the grid will not be stretched

- The upper and lower middle parts of the grid will be stretched horizontally

Image stretched horizontally from the centre

- The left and right middle parts of the grid will be stretched vertically

Image stretched vertically from the centre

And, the following is another case where the image is stretched both vertically and horizontally:

Image stretched both vertically and horizontally from the centre

This is a very useful property to achieve some specific behavior of texture, such as making a health bar in the game, where we don't want to stretch the corner side of the texture, so that if they are rounded, they should not be deformed.

Color

`SKSpriteNode` has some color properties too. Let's read in detail about them:

- `color`: This property is used to give color to a sprite. For example, you need to change the color of your sprite when the health bar is reduced to 50 percent, 25 percent, and so on.

- `colorBlendFactor`: This is used to control the color blending with the sprite texture. It can have a value between `0.0` to `1.0` (inclusive); `0.0` is default. If the value is `0.0`, that means the `color` property is ignored and texture values are used unmodified. If you increase the value, more color will be added to the sprite. For example, we can use this property to blend more color in our character with an increasing number of hits to the character:

Color effects due to change in value for colorBlendFactor

- `blendMode`: This property is used to blend sprites according to scene. Every pixel color of a sprite and the color of the corresponding scene pixel under it, is compared by Sprite Kit renderer to assign a resulting color to the sprite. This property is very useful when you add a lighting effect or flash effect to your scene.

In iOS 8, some lighting properties were added to generate a light and shadow effect on the sprites. Let's have a look at them:

- `lightingBitMask`: This property is used to show a lighting effect on the sprite, and is tested against light's `categoryBitMask` property by a logical AND operation. If the value is nonzero, the sprite will light up, or else it will remain unaffected by the light. Its default value is `0x00000000`.

- `shadowedBitMask`: This determines whether the sprite will be affected by the shadow generated by the light or not. This property is tested against light's `categoryBitMask` property by a logical AND operation. If the value is nonzero, the sprite will the drawn using a shadowed effect, or else it will remain unaffected by the light. Its default value is `0x00000000`.

- `shadowCastBitMask`: This determines whether or not the sprite will block the light and cast the shadow. This property is tested against light's `categoryBitMask` property by a logical AND operation. If the value is nonzero, the sprite will cast a shadow past itself, or else it will remain unaffected by the light. Its default value is `0x00000000`.

- `normalTexture`: A normal map texture is used when a sprite is lit, giving it a more realistic look with shadows and spectacular highlights. The texture must be a normal map texture.

Along with the lighting property, with iOS 8, the shader property was also introduced to customize the rendering effects.

Shader

The shader property is exclusively discussed in *Chapter 7, Particle Effects and Shaders*.

These are `SKSpriteNode` properties, by which we can use sprites by customizing them as we desire. The majority of a game consists of sprites, so it is important to know these properties and how we can use them. Now, it is time to use these properties in our game and see what effects they produce.

Adding a sprite without using textures

Mostly in a game, we add texture to our sprite, but we can also make a sprite without using textures. A texture property is an optional property in the `SKSpriteNode` class. If texture is nil, that means we have no texture to stretch, so the contract parameter is ignored. Let's open our `GameScene.swift` file and make a variable of `SKSpriteNode`, just below the `backgroundNode` declaration:

```
var spriteWithoutTexture : SKSpriteNode?
```

Now, with the preceding declaration, we have declared `spriteWithoutTexture` as optional. Since we have declared it optional, texture need not require a value. Now under `didMoveToView`, add following function:

```
func addSpriteWithoutTexture(){
  spriteWithoutTexture = SKSpriteNode(texture: nil, color:
  UIColor.redColor(), size: CGSizeMake(100, 100))
  addChild(spriteWithoutTexture!)
}
```

After that, call this function inside `didMoveToView()`, below the `addBackGround()` function:

```
addSpriteWithoutTexture()
```

Now tap on play and see what happens. In our `GameScene` there is no change. Well that's not what we desire. Actually, we missed the z position of our texture. That's why it is rendering behind the background and not showing to us. Add this line in our `addSpriteWithoutTexture()` function, before `addChild(spriteWithoutTexture!)`:

```
spriteWithoutTexture!.zPosition=1;
```

Run it. You will see a red square in the middle of the screen.

The code is self-explanatory. We made an instance of `SKSpriteNode` by instantiating it. We are passing nil as parameter for texture, meaning we don't want texture for this sprite. As we have made this sprite reference optional, we will have to unwrap it before using any `SKSpriteNode` properties, and we do so by using the `!` mark after `spriteWithoutTexture`.

We can also initialize in another way. Delete the `texture` parameter from the initialization part:

```
spriteWithoutTexture = SKSpriteNode(texture: nil, color:
UIColor.redColor(), size: CGSizeMake(100, 100))
```

Change the preceding initialization part as shown in the following:

```
spriteWithoutTexture = SKSpriteNode(color: UIColor.redColor(),
size: CGSizeMake(100, 100))
```

Run the code and it will produce the same result as the previous one. It automatically assigns nil to texture, and initializes a sprite with a color and the specified bounds. Let's do something interesting with it.

Changing the color property

We are going to use `color` property to change color when a user taps on this sprite. For this, first give a name to `spriteWithoutTexture`, so that we can recognize a tap on it:

```
spriteWithoutTexture!.name = "HELLO"
```

Add the following function in the `GameScene.swift` file to change color, as shown in the following code:

```
var
```

Now, we use the `touchesBegan` function to detect touch by a user (as it was used previously in the `MenuScene` class):

```
override func touchesBegan(touches: NSSet, withEvent event:
UIEvent) {
    for touch: AnyObject in touches{ currentno = 0;
func changeColor(){
    switch(currentno%3){
    case 0:
        spriteWithoutTexture!.color = UIColor.redColor()
    case 1:
        spriteWithoutTexture!.color = UIColor.greenColor()
    case 2:
        spriteWithoutTexture!.color = UIColor.blueColor()
    default :
        spriteWithoutTexture!.color = UIColor.blackColor()


    }
}


        let location = touch.locationInNode(self)
        let node = self.nodeAtPoint(location)
                if node.name == spriteWithoutTexture!.name {
                        currentno++
                        changeColor()
                }
    }
}
```

Now, after running Xcode, click on the colorful area in `GameScene`. You will see that area changing its color.

In this code, when a user taps on the sprite, it will add a value to the current one and call the `changeColor()` function. In the `changeColor()` function, we have taken a `switch` case to determine the color property of `spriteWithoutTexture`. In Swift, `switch` case is used as in many other languages. We don't have to use the `break` statement. Every `switch` statement must be *exhaustive*. That means, we have to make every single case check for switch case. Hence, we have to write a `default` value for every switch case.

If our texture is not nil, we can use the `colorBlendFactor` property to colorize the texture. We can use it for a tinting effect, such as damage taken in the game; `colorBlendFactor` is ignored if texture is nil. Its default value is `0.0`, which means that the texture should remain unmodified. When we increase the value, texture color is replaced with the blended color.

Changing colorBlendFactor in MenuScene

Let's add a tint to our play button. Open `MenuScene` and define a variable named `tintChanger` inside the `MenuScene` class as optional `Float`, so that we won't need to assign a value to it in the initializer:

```
var tintChanger : Float?
```

Add the following function in the `MenuScene` class:

```
func tintPlayButton(){
    if PlayButton.colorBlendFactor >= 1{
        tintChanger = -0.02
    }
    else if PlayButton.colorBlendFactor <= 0{
        tintChanger = 0.02
    }
    PlayButton.colorBlendFactor += CGFloat(tintChanger!)
}
```

Call it from the `update` function:

```
override func update(currentTime: NSTimeInterval) {
    tintPlayButton()
}
```

Now run Xcode. You will see the **Play** button appearing and disappearing respectively.

In this code, we just make a `Float` type variable. In our `tintPlayButton` function, we check if the value of its `colorBlendFactor` property is between 1 to 0.

Now let's give it a color, inside the `addChildToScene` function:

```
PlayButton.color = UIColor.redColor()
```

Run it and you will see the **Play** button changing its color from the original one to reddish. Now, it's time to see the position property in action.

Changing the position of a sprite

Now, have a look at the `position` property of `SKSpriteNode`. Let's open `GameScene` again, as we are going to see the `spriteWithoutTexture.position` property and the ways we can set it. Add this function below `changeColor`:

```
func changePosition(){
    switch(currentno%3){
```

```
    case 0:
        spriteWithoutTexture!.position = CGPointZero

    case 1:
        spriteWithoutTexture!.position =
CGPointMake(self.size.width/2-spriteWithoutTexture!.size.width/2,
0)
    case 2:
        spriteWithoutTexture!.position = CGPointMake
        (-self.size.width/2+spriteWithoutTexture!.size.width/2, 0)
    default :
        spriteWithoutTexture!.position = CGPointMake(0, 0)


    }
}
```

And call it just below the `changeColor()` call.

```
changePosition()
```

Now if you will run it and tap inside your game scene, you will see `spriteWithoutTexture` changing its position and toggling between them.

The most part of the code is the same as in `changecolor()`, except the position. In `case 0`, we set its position to `CGPointZero`. Position is measured in the `CGPoint` unit. `CGPointZero` is equivalent to `CGPointMake(0, 0)`. The position of a sprite depends on its `anchorPoint` as well as its parent `anchorPoint`.

As we define `GameScene anchorPoint` to `(0.5 , 0.5)`, it means any other node which will be added to `GameScene` will have the starting `position(0,0)`, from the middle of the screen. That's why the background and `spriteWithoutTexture` `(0,0)` co-ordinate will be in middle of the screen.

Now, as we specified the `anchorPoint` of `spriteWithoutTexture`, it will take its default value of `(0.5,0.5)`. This means that its `anchorPoint` will be in the center of it. Hence, in `case 0`, it is rendering in the middle of the screen symmetrically. In `case 1` and `case 2`, we just moved it to the right middle corner and left middle corner of the screen.

Let's try to change `anchorPoint` and see what happens. Add this line inside `addSpriteWithoutTexture`:

```
spriteWithoutTexture!.anchorPoint = CGPointZero
```

Now run it.

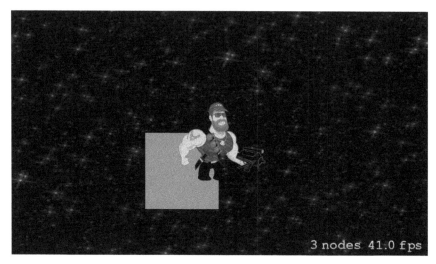

Before tap

After tap

You will see that all the positions are not as they were before. Can you guess the reason for this?

In the preceding code line, we assigned the new value (0,0) to spriteWithoutTexture, which will remove its default value (0.5,0.5). This means that its anchorPoint will not start from its middle. It will start from the bottom left of this. To visualize it, consider your sprite's top right corner as 1,1, and bottom left corner as 0,0. Now if you will set anchorPoint to 0,0, it will be at the bottom left of the sprite. If you will take it to 0,1, it will be at the top left. For 1,1, it will at the top right and for 1,0, it will at the bottom right. You can change it to whatever value you like, such as negative (-1,-2) and so on.

Now, we can see that setting anchorPoint becomes easy once we are familiar with co-ordinate numbers on the screen. So, let's test ourselves by setting the spriteWithoutTexture position to what it was before, using 0,0 as anchorPoint. Replace the changePosition function from this:

```
func changePosition(){
    switch(currentno%3){
    case 0:
        spriteWithoutTexture!.position = CGPointMake
(-spriteWithoutTexture!.size.width/2,
-spriteWithoutTexture!.size.height/2)

    case 1:
        spriteWithoutTexture!.position =
CGPointMake(self.size.width/2-spriteWithoutTexture!.size.width,
-spriteWithoutTexture!.size.height/2)
    case 2:
        spriteWithoutTexture!.position = CGPointMake
(-self.size.width/2, -spriteWithoutTexture!.size.height/2)
    default :
        spriteWithoutTexture!.position = CGPointMake(0, 0)

    }
}
```

Add the following line inside the addSpriteWithoutTexture() function:

```
spriteWithoutTexture!.position = CGPointMake
(-spriteWithoutTexture!.size.width/2,

-spriteWithoutTexture!.size.height/2)
```

Now run it. You will see the same result as before, in your GameScene.

In this code, we made a little adjustment. We want `spriteWithoutTexture` to be positioned in the center. As its `anchorPoint` is (0,0), its bottom left corner will be in the middle of the screen. So, to show it in the middle of the screen, we have to set its position by subtracting half of each width and height with the middle screen points, which are 0,0. Same goes for the left and right position of the `sprite`.

Now, just try to set `MenuScene anchorPoint` to (1,1), inside the `GameViewController.swift` file, and try to adjust the button and background position by yourself. If you are unable to do so, just add the following code inside the `addChildToScene` function:

```
 Background.position = CGPointMake(-self.size.width/2,
-self.size.height/2)
 PlayButton.position = CGPointMake(-self.size.width/2,

-self.size.height/2)
```

Now, if you run this code, you will notice the same result as before. After positioning, let's talk about resizing a sprite.

Resizing a sprite

As the `SKSpriteNode` class is inherited from the `SKNode` class, it also inherits `xScale` and `yScale` properties from the `SKNode` class. In our scene, we have given the background the same width as our view. We will achieve the same result as before, if we use its original size and scale its width and height. Open the `GameScene` class and update the `addBackGround` function as follows:

```
func addBackGround() {
    backgroundNode.zPosition = 0

    var scaleX =  self.size.width/backgroundNode.size.width
    var scaleY =  self.size.height/backgroundNode.size.height
    backgroundNode.xScale = scaleX
    backgroundNode.yScale = scaleY
    addChild(backgroundNode)
}
```

We have modified the function, `addBackGround()`. to enable our game to detect the screen dimensions of our device. This gives portability to our game (for example, the iPhone 5 and iPhone 6 have different screen dimensions). Now this function will return two float values as the ratio of screen size and background size in both width and height. After setting those to `backgroundNode.xScale` and `backgroundNode.yScale`, if you run this code, you will get the same result as before.

Working with texture objects

When a sprite is created, Sprite Kit creates a texture also. But sometime we require texture to do some complex work, such as:

- Changing the sprite
- Animation
- Using the same texture between multiple sprites
- Rendering a node tree into a texture like a screen shot

To make this simple, Sprite Kit provides us the SKTexture class. We can make an object of this class and use it as we want.

Open your MenuScene.swift file and make a reference of SKTexture:

```
let testingTexture : SKTexture
```

Now initialize it inside init code block

```
init(size:CGSize, playbutton:String, background:String) {
    PlayButton = SKSpriteNode(imageNamed: playbutton)
    Background = SKSpriteNode(imageNamed: background)
    MyPlayButton = SKSpriteNode(imageNamed: playbutton)
    testingTexture = SKTexture(imageNamed: playbutton)
    super.init(size:size)
}
```

Let's make a function call, generateTestTexture, and call it from didMoveToView:

```
override func didMoveToView(view: SKView) {
    addChildToScene();
    PlayButton.name = "PLAY"
    generateTestTexture()
}
    func generateTestTexture(){

        for var i = 0 ; i < 10; i++ {
            var temp = SKSpriteNode(texture: testingTexture)
            temp.xScale = 100/temp.size.width
            temp.yScale = 50/temp.size.height
            temp.zPosition = 2
            temp.position = CGPointMake(-self.size.width + CGFloat
(100 * i), -self.size.height/2)
            addChild(temp)
        }
    }
```

Run it and you will see many play textures in a sequence. We have made these using only one texture. Earlier, we were making the SKSpriteNode object from an image name, allowing Sprite Kit to create texture. Now we are assigning a texture to the SKNode object, which was created by us. Now, as we have done many customizations with sprites, let's have a look at the texture atlas.

What is a texture atlas?

A game's performance is dependent on the number of sprites used in it. The fewer the number of sprites, the more performance it gives. For this purpose, Sprite Kit provides texture atlases, which pack our image files automatically into one or more large images.

It provides us with a way to improve the performance of our game by drawing multiple images with a single draw call. When the game is in the development phase, compiler goes through every folder to find the folders with the *.atlas format. When those folders are identified, all of the images inside them are combined into one or more large image files. So, if you want to use this, place your images inside a folder and then rename it by suffixing .atlas to its name.

Now, we are going to add a player to GameScene. Let's take the player's all idle state images to a folder, and name it idle.atlas.

Now in Xcode, in **Project Navigator**, right-click on your project and select **Add to Project**:

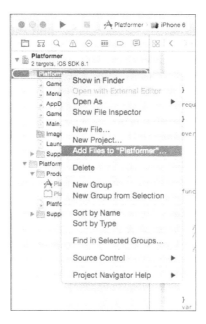

Select the directory (not the files) and click on **Add**. Defaults should be OK, but make sure it's set to copy.

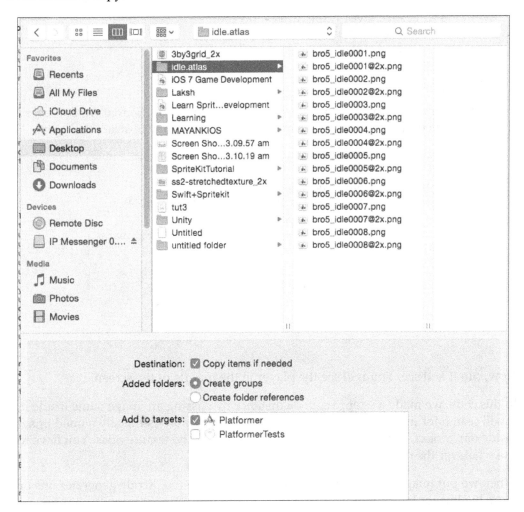

Now we are going to add a player to our `GameScene`. Open `GameScene` and create the function, `addPlayer`:

```
func addPlayer(){
    var player = SKSpriteNode(imageNamed:"bro5_idle0001")

    player.position = CGPoint(x:0,y:0)
    player.zPosition = 2;
    self.addChild(player)
}
```

Comment on the `addSpriteWithoutTexture` function and call the `addPlayer` function. Your function will look as follows:

```
override func didMoveToView(view: SKView) {
        addBackGround()
        //addSpriteWithoutTexture()
        addPlayer();
    }
```

Convert to comment tap part from `touchesBegan` in the code. So that we don't get stuck if a touch occurs; otherwise the image of the player may obstruct the touch:

```
override func touchesBegan(touches: NSSet, withEvent event:
UIEvent) {
        for touch: AnyObject in touches{
            let location = touch.locationInNode(self)
            let node = self.nodeAtPoint(location)
            // if node.name == spriteWithoutTexture!.name {
            //    currentno++
            //    changeColor()
            //    changePosition()

            //}
        }
    }
```

Now, run it and see. You will see the player in the middle of the screen.

In this code, we made a `SKSpriteNode` instance by passing an image name inside it. It will search for the Atlas for that image. But if we have an identically named image inside our project, this image will be loaded instead of the texture atlas. You have to use whatever the name of your image is.

When we put images inside a folder with `.atlas` extension, Xcode generates one or more big images by combining all the images into one.

1. To see that packed image, go to your `Products` folder in your project.
2. Right-click on the `.app` file there and click on **Show in Finder**, so that we can go to its directory.
3. Now, right-click on the `.app` file and select **Show Package Contents**.

4. After that, go to **Contents | Resources |** `*.atlasc`. Here you will see two files, an image, and a plist. If you will look at the image, you will find that images are combined into a texture, which has its height and width in the power of 2. If you will open the plist, you will see that it contains the position of images inside the packed texture, so that we can access them directly using Texture Atlas.

You can access texture atlas also. Let's use `TextureAtlas` and do something on tap:

1. First of all make a texture atlas reference in `GameScene`:

```
let myAtlas = SKTextureAtlas(named:"idle.atlas")
```

2. After that, make a player reference outside of function so that we can use it in another function too:

```
var player :SKSpriteNode?
```

3. Now edit the `addPlayer` function as follows:

```
func addPlayer(){
    player = SKSpriteNode(texture:
    myAtlas.textureNamed("bro5_idle0001"))
    player!.position = CGPoint(x:0,y:0)
    player!.zPosition = 2;
    player!.name = "Player"
    self.addChild(player!)
}
```

4. Make the function, `changeSpriteFromTextureAtlas()`, and call it from `touchesBegan`. Now, it should look like the following lines:

```
override func touchesBegan(touches: NSSet, withEvent event:
UIEvent) {
        for touch: AnyObject in touches{
            let location = touch.locationInNode(self)
            let node = self.nodeAtPoint(location)
            if node.name == player!.name {
                currentno++
                changeSpriteFromTextureAtlas()
            }
        }
    }
    func changeSpriteFromTextureAtlas(){
        switch(currentno%3){
        case 0:
            player!.texture = myAtlas.textureNamed("bro5_
idle0001")
```

```
        case 1:
                player!.texture = myAtlas.textureNamed("bro5_
    idle0004")
        case 2:
                player!.texture = myAtlas.textureNamed("bro5_
    idle0007")
        default :
            break

        }

    }
```

5. Now, run and tap on the player. You will see that the player changes its sprite on tap.

We have created the `SKTextureAtlas` reference. We named it as `atlas` file and added it to project. Now we can fetch the image from the texture atlas file. This is the way through which we can directly access the texture atlas. Texture atlases are very useful to make animation sequences or level generations from tiles. We will talk about animation in further chapters.

Now, as we are using textures to make sprites, sometimes we might need to preload textures into memory. Let's discuss this in detail.

Preloading textures into memory

Sprite Kit performs memory management very well. When a texture is needed to be rendered in scene, but is not prepared, Sprite Kit loads it into memory, and uploads it to the graphics hardware by converting it to a usable form. If many unloaded textures are needed at once, it might slow down the game. To avoid this, we need to preload textures before using them, especially in larger or more complex games.

This problem may arise when a user has to go from the level screen to the game screen. As the game screen may have many textures, it will need to load and might be slow due to the loading of texture. To avoid this, we can use the `SKTexture` class `preloadTextures(_:withCompletionHandler:)` function. It takes an array of SKTexture and a block, which is called after all the texture is loaded. So, we can use this block to load a scene.

For a small game, we can load all the textures at once, at game launch time. For a larger game, we will need to split the textures into different levels according to scene and other such criteria. The textures which are not useful to a level are discarded to save memory. And if the game is too big, we will need to load textures dynamically as the game runs.

As we load textures, we also need to remove the unnecessary textures from memory too. When a texture is loaded into memory, it stays there until its reference SKTexture object is deleted. To delete an SKTexture object, we have to remove the reference from it; this will make the texture unload from the memory.

Summary

In this chapter, we read about sprites in detail. We learned about how to initialize a sprite, and about the sizing and positioning of a sprite. We also learned about the various color properties of the sprite. The lighting and shader properties were also discussed. Finally, we discussed about the Texture object, usage of the texture atlas, and preloading of the texture into memory.

In the next chapter, we will be learning about nodes and various other concepts of the tree node structure.

4
Nodes in Sprite Kit

In the last chapter, we learnt about how to use sprites in a game in various ways. We discussed about the physical properties of sprites, textures of sprites, and various other properties, such as color property, lighting, shader, and so on. We also learned about working with texture objects and had an introduction to texture atlases.

In the previous chapter, we implemented the SKSprite class which is a subclass of the SKNode class; that's why SKSprite is a node itself, inheriting SKNode properties. In this chapter, we will study about nodes, which play an important role in understanding the tree structure of a game. Further, we will discuss about types of nodes in the Sprite Kit and their uses in detail.

All you need to know about nodes

We have discussed many things about nodes so far. Almost everything you are making in a game with Sprite Kit is a node. Scenes that we are presenting to view are instances of the SKScene class, which is a subclass of the SKEffectNode class, which is itself a subclass of the SKNode class. Indirectly, SKScene is a subclass of the SKNode class.

As a game follows the node tree formation, a scene acts like a root node and the other nodes are used as its children. It should be remembered that although SKNode is a base class for the node you see in a scene, it itself does not draw anything. It only provides some basic features to its subclass nodes. All the visual content we see in a Sprite Kit made game, is drawn by using the appropriate SKNode subclasses.

Following are some subclasses of SKNode classes, which are used for different behaviors in a Sprite Kit-based game:

- SKSpriteNode: This class is used to instantiate a texture sprite in the game; this is a familiar node class referred to frequently in *Chapter 3, Sprites*. SKVideoNode, this class is used to play video content in a scene.

- SKLabelNode: This class is used to draw labels in a game, with many customizing options, such as font type, font size, font color, and so on.

- SKShapeNode: This class is used to make a shape based on a path, at run time. For example, drawing a line or making a drawing game.

- SKEmitterNode: This class is used for emitting particle effects in a scene, with many options, such as position, number of particles, color, and so on.

- SKCropNode: This class is basically used for cropping its child nodes, using a mask. Using this, you can selectively block areas of a layer.

- SKEffectNode: SKEffectNode is the parent of the SKScene class and the subclass of the SKNode class. It is used for applying an image filter to its children.

- SKLightNode: SKLightNode class is used to make light and shadow effects in scene.

- SKFieldNode: This is a useful feature of Sprite Kit. You can define a portion of scene with some physical properties, for example, in space game, having a gravity effect on a black hole, which attracts the things which are nearby.

So, these are the basic subclasses of SKNode which are used frequently in Sprite Kit. SKNode provides some basic properties to its subclasses, which are used to view a node inside a scene, such as:

- position: This sets up the position of a node in a scene

- xScale: This scales in the width of a node

- yScale: This scales in the height of a node

- zRotation: This facilitates the rotation of a node in a clockwise or anti-clockwise direction

- frame: frame is a rectangle containing the nodes content along with its x-scale, y-scale and z-rotation properties, ignoring the nodes children

We know that the SKNode class does not draw anything by itself. So, what is the use of it? Well, we can use SKNode instances to manage our other nodes in different layers separately, or we can use them to manage different nodes in the same layer. Let's take a look at how we can do this.

Using the SKNode object in the game

Now, we will discover what the various aspects of SKNode are used for. Say you have to make a body from different parts of sprites, such as a car. You can make it from sprites of wheels and body. The wheels and body of a car run in synchronization with each other, so that one controls their action together, rather than manage each part separately. This can be done by adding them as a child of the SKNode class object and updating this node to control the activity of the car.

The SKNode class object can be used for layering purposes in a game. Suppose we have three layers in our game: the foreground layer, which represents foreground sprites, the middle layer, which represents the middle sprites, and the background layer which represents background sprites.

If we want a parallax effect in our game, we will have to update each sprite's position separately or we can make three SKNode objects, referring to each layer, and add the sprites to their respective nodes. Now we have to update only these three nodes' position and the sprites will update their position automatically.

The SKNode class can be used to make some kind of check point in a game, which is hidden but performs or triggers some event when a player crosses them, such as a level end, bonus, or death trap.

We can remove or add the whole sub tree inside a node and perform the necessary functions, such as rotating, scaling, positioning, and so on.

Well, as we described that we can use the SKNode object as checkpoints in the game, it is important to recognize them in your scene. So, how we do that? Well the SKNode class provides a property for this. Let's find out more about it.

Recognizing a node

The SKNode class provides a property with a name, to recognize the correct node. It takes string as a parameter. Either you can search a node by its name or you can use one of the two methods provided by SKNode, which are as follows:

- `func childNodeWithName(name:String) -> SKNode`: This function takes the name string as a parameter, and if it finds a node with a specific name, it returns that node or else it returns nil. If there is more than one node sharing the same name, it will return the first node in the search.

- func enumerateChildNodesWithName(name:String, usingBlock:((SKN ode!,UnsafeMutablePointer<ObjCBool>)->Void)!): When you need all the nodes sharing the same name, use this function. This function takes the name and block as a parameter. In usingBlock, you need to provide two parameters. One matching node, and the other a pointer of type Boolean. In our game, if you remember, we used the name property inside PlayButton to recognize the node when a user taps on it. It's a very useful property to search for the desired node.

So, let's have a quick look at other properties or methods of the SKNode class.

Initializing a node

There are two initializers to make an instance of SKNode. Both are available in iOS 8.0 or later.

- convenience init (fileNamed filename: String): This initializer is used for making a node by loading an archive file from main bundle. For this, you have to pass a file name with an sks extension in the main bundle.

- init(): It is used to make a simple node without any parameter. It is useful for layering purposes in a game.

As we already discussed the positioning of a node, let's discuss some functions and properties that are used to build a node tree.

Building a node tree

SKNode provides some functions and properties to work with a node tree. Following are some of the functions:

- addChild(node:SKNode): This is a very common function and is used mostly to make a node tree structure. We already used it to add nodes to scenes.

- insertChild(node:SKNode,atIndex index: Int): This is used when you have to insert a child in a specific position in the array.

- removeFromParent(): This simply removes a node from its parent.

- removeAllChildren(): This is used when you have to clear all the children in a node.

- removeChildrenInArray(nodes: [AnyObject]!): This takes an array of SKNode objects and removes it from the receiving node.

- `inParentHierarchy(parent:SKNode) -> Bool`: It takes an `SKNode` object to check as a parent of the receiving node, and returns a Boolean value according to that condition.

There are some useful properties used in a node tree, as follows:

- `children`: This is a read only property. It contains the receiving node's children in the array.
- `parent`: This is also a read only property. It contain the reference of the parent of the receiving node, and if there is none, then it returns nil.
- `scene`: This too is a read only property. If the node is embedded in the scene, it will contain the reference of the scene, otherwise nil.

In a game, we need some specific task on a node, such as changing its position from one point to another, changing sprites in a sequence, and so on. These tasks are done using actions on node. Let's talk about them now.

Actions on a node tree

Actions are required for some specific tasks in a game. For this, the `SKNode` class provides some basic functions, which are as follows.

- `runAction(action:SKAction!)`: This function takes an `SKAction` class object as a parameter and performs the action on the receiving node.
- `runAction(action:SKAction!,completion block: (() -> Void)!)`: This function takes an `SKAction` class object and a compilation block as object. When the action completes, it calls the block.
- `runAction(action:SKAction,withKey key:String!)`: This function takes an `SKAction` class object and a unique key, to identify this action and perform it on the receiving node.
- `actionForKey(key:String) -> SKAction?`: This takes a `String` key as a parameter and returns an associative `SKAction` object for that key identifier. This happens if it exists, otherwise it returns nil.
- `hasActions() -> Bool`: Through this action, if the node has any executing action, it returns `true`, or else `false`.
- `removeAllActions()`: This function removes all actions from the receiving node.
- `removeActionForKey(key:String)`: This takes `String` name as key and removes an action associated with that key, if it exists.

Some useful properties to control these actions are as follows:

- `speed`: This is used to speed up or speed down the action motion. The default value is `1.0` to run at normal speed; with increasing value, speed increases.

- `paused`: This Boolean value determines whether an action on the node should be paused or resumed.

Sometimes, we require changing a point coordinate system according to a node inside a scene. The `SKNode` class provides two functions to interchange a point's coordinate system with respect to a node in a scene. Let's talk about them.

The coordinate system of a node

We can convert a point with respect to the coordinate system of any node tree. The functions to do that, are as follows:

- `convertPoint(point:CGPoint, fromNode node : SKNode) -> CGPoint`: This takes a point in another node's coordinate system and the other node as its parameter, and returns a converted point according to the receiving node's coordinate system.

- `convertPoint(point:CGPoint, toNode node:SKNode) ->CGPoint`: It takes a point in the receiving node's coordinate system and the other nodes in the node tree as its parameters, and returns the same point converted according to the other node's coordinate system.

We can also determine if a point is inside a node's area or not.

- `containsPoint(p:CGPoint) -> Bool`: This returns the Boolean value according to the position of a point inside or outside of a receiving node's bounding box.

- `nodeAtPoint(p:CGPoint) -> SKNode`: This returns the deepest descendant node that intersects the point. If that is not there, then it returns the receiver node.

- `nodesAtPoint(p:CGPoint) -> [AnyObject]`: This returns an array of all the `SKNode` objects in the subtree that intersect the point. If no nodes intersect the point, an empty array is returned.

Apart from these, the `SKNode` class provides some other functions and properties too. Let's talk about them.

Other functions and properties

Some other functions and properties of the SKNode class are as follows:

- intersectsNode(node:SKNode) -> Bool: As the name suggests, it returns a Boolean value according to the intersection of the receiving node and another node from the function parameter.

- physicsBody: It is a property of the SKNode class. The default value is nil, which means that this node will not take part in any physical simulation in the scene. If it contains any physical body, then it will change its position and rotation in accordance with the physical simulation in the scene.

- userData : NSMutableDictionary?: The userData property is used to store data for a node in a dictionary form. We can store position, rotation, and many custom data sets about the node inside it.

- constraints: [AnyObject]?: It contains an array of constraints SKConstraint objects to the receiving node. Constraints are used to limit the position or rotation of a node inside a scene.

- reachConstraints: SKReachConstraints?: This is basically used to make restricted values for the receiving node by making an SKReachConstraints object. For example, to make joints move in a human body.

- Node blending modes: The SKNode class declares an enum SKBlendMode of the int type to blend the receiving node's color by using source and destination pixel colors. The constant's used for this are as follows:

  ○ Alpha: It is used to blend source and destination colors by multiplying the source alpha value

  ○ Add: It is used to add the source and destination colors

  ○ Subtract: It is used to subtract the source color from the destination color

  ○ Multiply: It is used to multiply the source color by the destination color

  ○ MultiplyX2: It is used to multiply the source color by the destination color, and after that, the resulting color is doubled

  ○ Screen: It is used to multiply the inverted source and the destination color respectively and it then inverts the final result color

  ○ Replace: It is used to replace the destination color by source color

- calculateAccumulatedFrame()->CGRect: We know that a node does not draw anything by itself, but if a node has descendants that draw content, then we may be required to know the overall frame size of that node. This function calculates the frame that contains the content of the receiver node and all of its descendants.

Now, we are ready to see some basic `SKNode` subclasses in action. The classes we are going to discuss are as follows:

- `SKLabelNode`
- `SKCropNode`
- `SKShapeNode`
- `SKEmitterNode`
- `SKLightNode`
- `SKVideoNode`

To study these classes, we are going to create six different `SKScene` subclasses in our project, so that we can learn them separately.

Now, having learned in detail about nodes, we can proceed further to utilize the concept of nodes in a game.

Creating subclasses for our Platformer game

With the theoretical understanding of nodes, one wonders how this concept is helpful in developing a game. To understand the development of a game using the concept of Nodes, we now go ahead with writing and executing code for our *Platformer* game.

Create the subclasses of different nodes in Xcode, following the given steps:

1. From the main menu, select **New File** | **Swift** | **Save As** | **NodeMenuScene. swift**:

    Make sure **Platformer** is ticked as the target. Now **Create** and **Open** and make the `NodeMenuScene` class by subclassing `SKScene`.

2. Following the previous same steps as, make `CropScene`, `ShapeScene`, `ParticleScene`, `LightScene`, and `VideoNodeScene` files, respectively.

3. Open the `GameViewController.swift` file and replace the `viewDidLoad` function by typing out the following code:

```
override func viewDidLoad() {
        super.viewDidLoad()

        let menuscene = NodeMenuScene()
```

```
let skview = view as SKView

skview.showsFPS = true
skview.showsNodeCount = true
skview.ignoresSiblingOrder = true
menuscene.scaleMode = .ResizeFill

menuscene.anchorPoint = CGPoint(x: 0.5, y: 0.5)
menuscene.size = view.bounds.size
skview.presentScene(menuscene)

    }
```

In this code, we just called our NodeMenuScene class from the GameViewController class. Now, it's time to add some code to the NodeMenuScene class.

NodeMenuScene

Open the NodeMenuScene.swift file and type in the code as shown next. Do not worry about the length of the code; as this code is for creating the node menu screen, most of the functions are similar to creating buttons:

```
import Foundation
import SpriteKit

let BackgroundImage = "BG"
let FontFile = "Mackinaw1"

let sKCropNode = "SKCropNode"

let sKEmitterNode = "SKEmitterNode"

let sKLightNode = "SKLightNode"
let sKShapeNode = "SKShapeNode"
let sKVideoNode = "SKVideoNode"
class NodeMenuScene: SKScene {

    let transitionEffect = SKTransition.
flipHorizontalWithDuration(1.0)
    var labelNode : SKNode?
    var backgroundNode : SKNode?
```

```
override func didMoveToView(view: SKView) {
    backgroundNode = getBackgroundNode()
    backgroundNode!.zPosition = 0
    self.addChild(backgroundNode!)
    labelNode = getLabelNode()
    labelNode?.zPosition = 1
    self.addChild(labelNode!)


}
    func getBackgroundNode() -> SKNode {
    var bgnode = SKNode()
    var bgSprite = SKSpriteNode(imageNamed: "BG")
    bgSprite.xScale = self.size.width/bgSprite.size.width
    bgSprite.yScale = self.size.height/bgSprite.size.height
    bgnode.addChild(bgSprite)
    return bgnode
}
func getLabelNode() -> SKNode {
var labelNode = SKNode()
    var cropnode = SKLabelNode(fontNamed: FontFile)
    cropnode.fontColor = UIColor.whiteColor()
    cropnode.name = sKCropNode
    cropnode.text = sKCropNode
    cropnode.position =
CGPointMake(CGRectGetMinX(self.frame)+cropnode.frame.width/2,
CGRectGetMaxY(self.frame)-cropnode.frame.height)
    labelNode.addChild(cropnode)
    var emitternode = SKLabelNode(fontNamed: FontFile)
    emitternode.fontColor = UIColor.blueColor()
    emitternode.name = sKEmitterNode
    emitternode.text = sKEmitterNode
    emitternode.position =
CGPointMake(CGRectGetMinX(self.frame) + emitternode.frame.width/2
, CGRectGetMidY(self.frame) - emitternode.frame.height/2)
    labelNode.addChild(emitternode)

    var lightnode = SKLabelNode(fontNamed: FontFile)
    lightnode.fontColor = UIColor.whiteColor()
    lightnode.name = sKLightNode
    lightnode.text = sKLightNode
    lightnode.position = CGPointMake(CGRectGetMaxX(self.frame)
- lightnode.frame.width/2 , CGRectGetMaxY(self.frame) -
lightnode.frame.height)
```

```
        labelNode.addChild(lightnode)

        var shapetnode = SKLabelNode(fontNamed: FontFile)
        shapetnode.fontColor = UIColor.greenColor()
        shapetnode.name = sKShapeNode
        shapetnode.text = sKShapeNode
        shapetnode.position =
CGPointMake(CGRectGetMaxX(self.frame) - shapetnode.frame.width/2 ,
CGRectGetMidY(self.frame) - shapetnode.frame.height/2)
        labelNode.addChild(shapetnode)

        var videonode = SKLabelNode(fontNamed: FontFile)
        videonode.fontColor = UIColor.blueColor()
        videonode.name = sKVideoNode
        videonode.text = sKVideoNode
        videonode.position = CGPointMake(CGRectGetMaxX(self.frame)
- videonode.frame.width/2 , CGRectGetMinY(self.frame) )
        labelNode.addChild(videonode)

        return labelNode
    }
    var once:Bool = true
    override func touchesBegan(touches: NSSet, withEvent event:
    UIEvent) {
        if !once {
            return
        }
        for touch: AnyObject in touches {
            let location = touch.locationInNode(self)
            let node = self.nodeAtPoint(location)
            if node.name == sKCropNode {
                once = false
                var scene = CropScene()
                scene.anchorPoint = CGPointMake(0.5, 0.5)
                scene.scaleMode = .ResizeFill
                scene.size = self.size
                self.view?.presentScene(scene,
                transition:transitionEffect)
            }

            else if node.name == sKEmitterNode {
                once = false
                var scene = ParticleScene()
                scene.anchorPoint = CGPointMake(0.5, 0.5)
                scene.scaleMode = .ResizeFill
```

```
                scene.size = self.size
                self.view?.presentScene(scene,
                transition:transitionEffect)
            }
            else if node.name == sKLightNode {
                once = false
                var scene = LightScene()
                scene.scaleMode = .ResizeFill
                scene.size = self.size
                scene.anchorPoint = CGPointMake(0.5, 0.5)
                self.view?.presentScene(scene ,
                transition:transitionEffect)
            }
            else if node.name == sKShapeNode {
                once = false
                var scene = ShapeScene()
                scene.scaleMode = .ResizeFill
                scene.size = self.size

                scene.anchorPoint = CGPointMake(0.5, 0.5)
                self.view?.presentScene(scene,
                transition:transitionEffect)
            }
            else if node.name == sKVideoNode {
                once = false
                var scene = VideoNodeScene()
                scene.scaleMode = .ResizeFill
                scene.size = self.size
                scene.anchorPoint = CGPointMake(0.5, 0.5)
                self.view?.presentScene(scene ,
                transition:transitionEffect)
            }
        }
    }
}
```

We will get the following screen from the previous code:

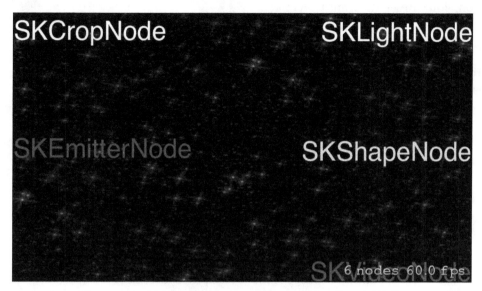

The screen is obtained when we execute the NodeMenuScene.swift file

In the preceding code, after `import` statements, we defined some `String` variables. We are going to use these variables as `Label` names in the scene .We also added our font name as a string variable. Inside this class, we made two node references: one for background and the other for those labels which we are going to use in this scene. We are using these two nodes to make layers in our game. It is best to categorize the nodes in a scene, so that we can optimize the code. We make an `SKTransition` object reference of the flip horizontal effect. You can use other transition effects too.

Inside the `didMoveToView()` function, we just get the node and add it to our scene and set their z position.

Now, if we look at the `getBackgroundNode()` function, we can see that we made a node by the `SKNode` class instance, a background by the `SKSpriteNode` class instance, and then added it to the node and returned it. If you see the syntax of this function, you will see `-> SKNode`. It means that this function returns an `SKNode` object.

The same goes in the function, `getLabelNode()`. It also returns a node containing all the `SKLabelNode` class objects. We have given a font and a name to these labels and set the position of them in the screen. The `SKLabelNode` class is used to make labels in Sprite Kit with many customizable options.

In the `touchBegan()` function, we get the information on which Label is touched, and we then call the appropriate scene with transitions.

With this, we have created a scene with the transition effect. By tapping on each button, you can see the transition effect.

CropScene

In this scene, we are going to use the SKCropNode class object. This class is used to mask one node on another. We are going to use our play sprite as a mask and our background image as an image that is to be rendered according to the masking area. Open the CropScene.swift file and type in the code, as shown next:

```
import Foundation
import SpriteKit
class CropScene : SKScene {
    var play : SKSpriteNode?
    override func didMoveToView(view: SKView) {
        play = SKSpriteNode(imageNamed: "Play")
        var crop = SKCropNode()
        crop.maskNode = play
        crop.addChild(SKSpriteNode(imageNamed: "BG"))
        addChild(crop)
        addBackLabel()
    }
    func addBackLabel() {
        var backbutton = SKLabelNode(fontNamed: FontFile)
        backbutton.fontColor = UIColor.blueColor()
        backbutton.name = "BACK"
        backbutton.text = "BACK"
        backbutton.position =
CGPointMake(CGRectGetMinX(self.frame) + backbutton.frame.width/2 ,
CGRectGetMinY(self.frame))
        self.addChild(backbutton)
    }
    var once:Bool = true
    override func touchesBegan(touches: NSSet, withEvent event:
    UIEvent) {
        for touch: AnyObject in touches {
            let location = touch.locationInNode(self)
            let node = self.nodeAtPoint(location)
            if node.name == "BACK" {
                if once {
                    once = false
                    let transitionEffect =
                    SKTransition.flipHorizontalWithDuration(1.0)
                    var scene = NodeMenuScene()
```

```
                    scene.anchorPoint = CGPointMake(0.5, 0.5)
                    scene.scaleMode = .ResizeFill
                    scene.size = self.size
                    self.view?.presentScene(scene,
                    transition:transitionEffect)
                }
            }
        }
    }
}
```

We will get the following screen, with the preceding code:

The preceding screen is obtained when we execute the Cropscene.swift file

In this code, we just added a label for the back press of the SKLabelNode class object.

In this class, we added play image to the mask node of the SKCropNode object and added a background to this crop node. If you click on the SKCropNode label in the NodeMenuScene, you will see that the play image is working as a mask over the background image.

ShapeScene

Now, open the ShapeScene.swift file and add the following code to create the SKShapeNode class:

```
import Foundation
import SpriteKit
class ShapeScene : SKScene {
```

```
        override func didMoveToView(view: SKView) {

                var shape = SKShapeNode()
                var path = CGPathCreateMutable()
                CGPathMoveToPoint(path, nil, 0, 0)
            CGPathAddLineToPoint(path, nil, 10  , 100)
            CGPathAddLineToPoint(path, nil, 20, 0)
            CGPathAddLineToPoint(path, nil, 10, -10)
            CGPathAddLineToPoint(path, nil, 0, 0)
            shape.path = path
            shape.fillColor = UIColor.redColor()
            shape.lineWidth = 4
            addChild(shape)
            addBackLabel()
        }
    func addBackLabel() {
        var backbutton = SKLabelNode(fontNamed: FontFile)
        backbutton.fontColor = UIColor.blueColor()
        backbutton.name = "BACK"
        backbutton.text = "BACK"
        backbutton.position =
CGPointMake(CGRectGetMinX(self.frame) + backbutton.frame.width/2 ,
CGRectGetMinY(self.frame))
        self.addChild(backbutton)
    }
    var once:Bool = true
    override func touchesBegan(touches: NSSet, withEvent event:
    UIEvent) {
        for touch: AnyObject in touches {
            let location = touch.locationInNode(self)
            let node = self.nodeAtPoint(location)
            if node.name == "BACK" {
                if once {
                    once = false
                    let transitionEffect =
                    SKTransition.flipHorizontalWithDuration(1.0)
                    var scene = NodeMenuScene()
                    scene.anchorPoint = CGPointMake(0.5, 0.5)
                    scene.scaleMode = .ResizeFill
                    scene.size = self.size
                    self.view?.presentScene(scene,
                    transition:transitionEffect)
                }
            }
        }
    }
}
```

We will get the following screen with the previous code:

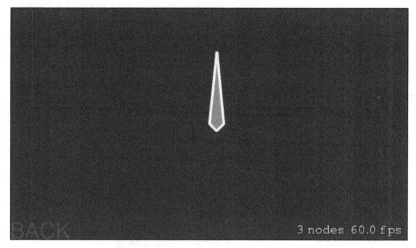

This screen is obtained when we execute the ShapeScene.swift file

The `SKShapeNode` class is basically used to make runtime graphics in scene. In this example, we have created a drawing of four lines and then filled it with a color by using the `fillColor` property.

ParticleScene

Now, open the `ParticleScene.swift` file and add the following code to create the `SKEmitterNode` class:

```
import Foundation.
import SpriteKit
class ParticleScene : SKScene {
    var emitternode :SKEmitterNode?
    override func didMoveToView(view: SKView) {
    var path =
NSBundle.mainBundle().pathForResource("MagicParticle", ofType:
"sks")
    emitternode = NSKeyedUnarchiver.unarchiveObjectWithFile(path!)
as? SKEmitterNode
        self.addChild(emitternode!)
   addBackLabel()
    }
    func addBackLabel() {
        var backbutton = SKLabelNode(fontNamed: FontFile)
        backbutton.fontColor = UIColor.blueColor()
        backbutton.name = "BACK"
```

```
        backbutton.text = "BACK"
        backbutton.position =
CGPointMake(CGRectGetMinX(self.frame) + backbutton.frame.width/2 ,
CGRectGetMinY(self.frame))
        self.addChild(backbutton)
    }
  var once:Bool = true
  override func touchesBegan(touches: NSSet, withEvent event:
  UIEvent) {
        for touch:AnyObject in touches {
            var location = touch.locationInNode(self)
            emitternode?.position = location
            let node = self.nodeAtPoint(location)
             if node.name == "BACK" {
                 if once {
                     once = false
                     let transitionEffect =
                     SKTransition.flipHorizontalWithDuration(1.0)
                     var scene = NodeMenuScene()
                     scene.anchorPoint = CGPointMake(0.5, 0.5)
                     scene.scaleMode = .ResizeFill
                     scene.size = self.size
                     self.view?.presentScene(scene,
                     transition:transitionEffect)
                 }
             }
        }
    }
  }
}
```

We get the following screen with the previous code:

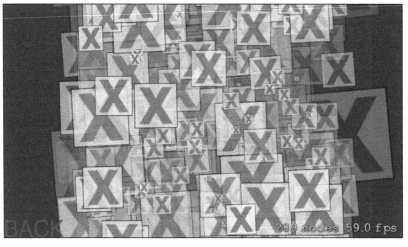

This screen is obtained when we execute the ParticleScene.swift file

We used the SKEmitterNode class object for the particle effect. Sprite Kit gives you many predefined particle effects. You can customize them according to your requirements. To make a particle effect, follow these steps:

1. Right click on project explorer, **New File | Resource | SpriteKit Particle File**.

2. Choose a particle template from the list and then click on **Next**.

3. **Save As**, name your particle system. We named it MagicParticle, in our project. Make sure that in the **Targets** option, the **Platformer** (project) is selected before you click on the **Create** button.

In the **Project Navigator**, on the left side of screen, you will see the MagicParticle. sks file. If you click on this file, you can see the particle effect in the editor window. Now, on the right side panel, many options are available for particle, color, shape, and so on. You can select any value as per your liking.

LightScene

Now, open the LightScene.swift file and add the following code to create the SKLightNode class:

```
import Foundation
import SpriteKit
class LightScene : SKScene {
    var lightNode : SKLightNode?
    override func didMoveToView(view: SKView) {
        var background = SKSpriteNode(imageNamed: "BG")
        background.zPosition = 0.5
        var scaleX =  self.size.width/background.size.width
        var scaleY =  self.size.height/background.size.height
        background.xScale = scaleX
        background.yScale = scaleY
        addChild(background)
        println(background.size)
        var playbutton = SKSpriteNode(imageNamed: "Play")
        playbutton.zPosition = 1
        playbutton.size = CGSizeMake(100, 100)
        playbutton.position = CGPointMake(-200, 0)
        addChild(playbutton)
        var playbutton2 = SKSpriteNode(imageNamed: "Play")
        playbutton2.zPosition = 1
        playbutton2.size = CGSizeMake(100, 100)
        playbutton2.position = CGPointMake(0, 100)
        addChild(playbutton2)
```

```
        var playbutton3 = SKSpriteNode(imageNamed: "Play")
        playbutton3.zPosition = 1
        playbutton3.size = CGSizeMake(100, 100)
        playbutton3.position = CGPointMake(200, 0)
        addChild(playbutton3)
        lightNode = SKLightNode()
        lightNode!.categoryBitMask = 1
        lightNode!.falloff = 1
        lightNode!.ambientColor = UIColor.greenColor()
        lightNode!.lightColor = UIColor.redColor()
        lightNode!.shadowColor = UIColor.blueColor()
        lightNode!.zPosition = 1
        addChild(lightNode!)
        playbutton.shadowCastBitMask = 1
        playbutton2.shadowCastBitMask = 1
        playbutton3.shadowCastBitMask = 1
        background.lightingBitMask = 1;
        addBackLabel()
    }
    func addBackLabel() {
        var backbutton = SKLabelNode(fontNamed: FontFile)
        backbutton.fontColor = UIColor.blueColor()
        backbutton.name = "BACK"
        backbutton.text = "BACK"
        backbutton.position = CGPointMake(CGRectGetMinX(self.frame) +
backbutton.frame.width/2 ,
CGRectGetMinY(self.frame))
        backbutton.zPosition = 3
        self.addChild(backbutton)
    }
    var once:Bool = true
    override func touchesMoved(touches: NSSet, withEvent event:
    UIEvent) {
        for touch : AnyObject in touches {
            let location = touch.locationInNode(self)
            lightNode!.position = location
            let node = self.nodeAtPoint(location)
            if node.name == "BACK" {
                if once {
                    once = false
                    let transitionEffect =
                    SKTransition.flipHorizontalWithDuration(1.0)
                    var scene = NodeMenuScene()
                    scene.anchorPoint = CGPointMake(0.5, 0.5)
                    scene.scaleMode = .ResizeFill
```

```
                    scene.size = self.size
                    self.view?.presentScene(scene,
                    transition:transitionEffect)
                }
            }
        }
    }
}
```

We will get the following screen, using the preceding code:

The preceding screen is obtained when we execute the LightScene.swift file

In this class, we used a light source and set bitmasks to images. If you run the project, you will see that the background color is being affected by the lighting source, and other play images are casting shadows in the opposite direction. If you click on scene, the lighting source will change its position and shadows will also change themselves according to the source.

VideoNodeScene

Now, open the VideoNodeScene.swift file and add the following code to create the SKVideoNode class:

```
import Foundation
import SpriteKit
import AVFoundation
class VideoNodeScene : SKScene {
    var playonce :Bool = false
    var videoNode : SKVideoNode?
```

```
override func didMoveToView(view: SKView) {
    var background = SKSpriteNode(imageNamed: "BG")
    background.zPosition = 0
    var scaleX =  self.size.width/background.size.width
    var scaleY =  self.size.height/background.size.height
    background.xScale = scaleX
    background.yScale = scaleY
    addChild(background)
    var fileurl =
NSURL.fileURLWithPath(NSBundle.mainBundle().pathForResource
("Movie", ofType: "m4v")!)
    var player = AVPlayer(URL: fileurl)
    videoNode = SKVideoNode(AVPlayer: player)
    videoNode?.size = CGSizeMake(200, 150)
    videoNode?.zPosition = 1
    videoNode?.name = "Video"
    self.addChild(videoNode!)
    addBackLabel()
}
func addBackLabel() {
    var backbutton = SKLabelNode(fontNamed: FontFile)
    backbutton.fontColor = UIColor.blueColor()
    backbutton.name = "BACK"
    backbutton.text = "BACK"
    backbutton.position =
CGPointMake(CGRectGetMinX(self.frame) + backbutton.frame.width/2 ,
CGRectGetMinY(self.frame))

    self.addChild(backbutton)
}
var once:Bool = true
override func touchesBegan(touches: NSSet, withEvent event:
UIEvent) {
    for touch: AnyObject in touches {
        let location = touch.locationInNode(self)
        let node = self.nodeAtPoint(location)
        if node.name == videoNode?.name {
            if !playonce {
                videoNode?.play()
                playonce = true
            }

        }
        if node.name == "BACK" {
            if once {
```

```
once = false
let transitionEffect =
SKTransition.flipHorizontalWithDuration(1.0)
var scene = NodeMenuScene()
scene.anchorPoint = CGPointMake(0.5, 0.5)
scene.scaleMode = .ResizeFill
scene.size = self.size
self.view?.presentScene(scene,
transition:transitionEffect)
        }
    }
 }
 }


}
```

We will get the following screen:

The preceding screen is obtained when we execute the LightScene.swift file

To use audio and video in our scene, we have imported `AVFoundation` into our code. We have added a video file with the `.m4v` format in our project. We have used a file named `Movie.a4v` for this project. So, we are done with the coding part for this chapter. We learned six majorly used subclasses of `SKNode`.

Summary

In this chapter, we learned about nodes in detail. We discussed many properties and functions of the SKNode class of Sprite Kit, along with its usage. Also, we discussed about the building of a node tree, and actions on a node tree. Now we are familiar with the major subclasses of SKNode, namely SKLabelNode, SKCropNode, SKShapeNode, SKEmitterNode, SKLightNode, and SKVideoNode, along with their implementation in our game.

In the next chapter, we will learn the basics of adding physics simulation in a Sprite Kit game. We will also learn about adding physics to the different nodes in our game.

5
Physics in Sprite Kit

In previous chapters, we had gone through essentials to develop a game in Sprite Kit. Also, we have already developed starting scenes, which are different screen views associated with menu items.

To recap the previous chapter, where we discussed about nodes in detail, we studied the `SKNode` class and its associated properties and functions. Along with this, we discussed about building a node tree and actions on a node tree. We also applied major subclasses in our game, such as `SKLabelNode`, `SKCropNode`, `SKShapeNode`, `SKEmitterNode`, `SKLightNode`, and `SKVideoNode` to create the menu scene. Now, the time has come to venture further into Sprite Kit.

In the real world we are affected by many physical laws, such as mass, gravity, velocity, and so on. To make a game more realistic, Sprite Kit provides us with some classes and functions, which are used to make nodes act like bodies as in a real environment. By applying these classes to characters, environment, and so on, our game becomes realistic.

For example, in a platform game which involves a player walking on a road. It will be better to have gravity, force, friction, and so on, being applied to the player, the road or any other obstacle. Now, we are going to discuss about simulating physics in our game *Platformer*.

Simulating physics in Sprite Kit

Most of the game engines have an inbuilt physics engine, and you can also add an external physics engine to a game engine. Fortunately, Apple provides a physics engine in Sprite Kit. In Sprite Kit, physics properties are applied by an object of the class, `SKPhysicsBody`. As we have already learned that objects are connected to a node in a node tree, physics simulation uses a node's orientation and position for simulation. In Sprite Kit, when a game renders, each frame invokes some functions in a cycle, as follows:

```
update
didEvaluateActions
didSimulatePhysics
didApplyConstraints
didFinishUpdate
```

After actions (such as image changing in a node for animation) `SKScene` simulates physics to do all the actions, such as gravity on a physics body, velocity change, collision between two physics bodies, and so on. If we go through our `SKNode` class, we will see there is a property called `physicsBody`. It takes the `SKPhysicsBody` object as a parameter and defines physics laws on those objects; it is obvious it will be inherited from its subclasses, such as `SKSpriteNode`, `SKEmitterNode`, `SKVideoNode`, and more. So, we can make any `SKNode` subclass a physics body by setting the `physicsBody` property on it.

Now it is time to dive into some necessary documentation of the essential class responsible for the physics behavior of a node in a scene. Let's discuss about the `SKPhysicsBody` class.

SKPhysicsBody

A node's `physicsBody` property uses the `SKPhysicsBody` class object. In the life cycle of a frame, the `didSimulatePhysics` function is called just after actions are evaluated. The work of this function is to calculate the physical properties, such as gravity, velocity, friction, restitution, collision, or other forces. After these calculations are done, the positions and orientations of nodes are updated in the `update` function. If we are going to apply some force on a node, it is necessary that we assign the `SKPhysicsBody` object to that node first.

Sprite Kit provides us with two kinds of physics bodies:

- **Volume-based**: These are the kind of physics bodies that have mass and volume

- **Edge-based**: These are the kind of physics bodies that don't have mass and volume

In volume-based bodies, we can control if it should be affected by gravity, friction, collision, and so on, by setting it as `static` or `dynamic`. This property is very useful as we can make a static platform or a moving object by just tweaking this property. These bodies are defined within specified boundaries, such as circle, rectangle, polygon, and so on. Irregular shapes are not allowed. For an irregular shaped body one can join small volume-based bodies to achieve desired pattern for a physics object.

On the other hand, edge-based bodies are used to make volume-less spaces in the game scene. That means they are not solid and allow other physics body inside their own boundaries. Edge-based physics bodies are always treated as if their `dynamic` property is `false` and could collide only with other volume-based physics bodies. To understand the concept of edge-based body, think of a scene having clouds; a cloud can never be solid, a volume-based physics object can enter into it.

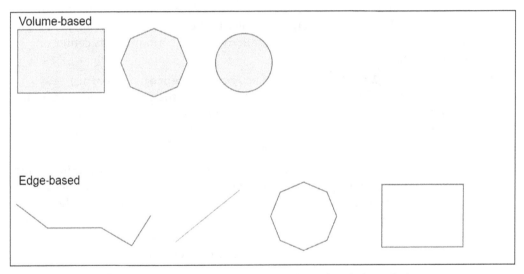

A graphical example of volume-based and edge-based physics bodies

These two kinds of physics bodies are made by calling appropriate initialization of `SKPhysicsBody`. We mostly use volume-based physics bodies in our scene.

As we define that, we need to instantiate the `SKPhysicsBody` class for making volume-based or edge-based physics bodies.

The initialization of volume-based physics bodies

Following are the initializers for volume-based physics bodies:

- `init(circleOfRadius r: CGFloat) -> SKPhysicsBody`: This initializer is used to make a circular physics body. It takes radius as a parameter and returns an `SKPhysicsBody` object. The center of gravity of this body lies in the center of the receiving node, that is, the, node on which this function is applied.

- `init(circleOfRadius r: CGFloat,center center: CGPoint) -> SKPhysicsBody`: This initializer is very similar to the previous one except in that it takes one more parameter, that is, the origin of the physics body. We can shift our gravity or circular physics body's center with respect to the receiving coordinate system assigned by this initializer.

- `init!(rectangleOfSize s: CGSize) -> SKPhysicsBody`: This initializer is used to make rectangle shaped physics bodies. It takes a `rectangle` as a parameter and returns an `SKPhysicsBody` object, containing its center on the receiving node's center.

- `init!(rectangleOfSize s: CGSize,center center: CGPoint) -> SKPhysicsBody`: This initializer is very similar to the previous one except in that it takes one more parameter that is, origin of the physics body. We can shift gravity on a rectangular physics body to the center with respect to the receiving coordinate system assigned by this initializer.

- `init(bodies bodies: [AnyObject]) -> SKPhysicsBody`: This initializer is used to make a new physics body by using the array of existing physics bodies. For this we have to pass only volume-based physics body objects in the array. The resultant area of the physics body from this initializer, is the union of the other child physics body inside the array. As it uses the shapes of its children's bodies, it means it can have spaces inside it, or even blank fields.

- `init!(polygonFromPath path: CGPath!) -> SKPhysicsBody`: This initializer is used to make a polygon shaped physics body. It takes a convex polygon path with counterclockwise winding as a parameter.

- `init!(texture texture: SKTexture!,size size: CGSize) -> SKPhysicsBody`: This initializer is used to make a physics body using a texture. This is used when we need a physics body shape as per the texture shape. It is called per pixel physics and is very useful when the shape is neither rectangular nor circular. It was introduced in iOS 8. In this initializer, a texture and a size are used as parameters. First, texture is scaled to that size and then, the shape of the newly created physics body is decided by all of the pixels having a non-zero alpha value.

- `init!(texture texture: SKTexture!,alphaThreshold alphaThreshold: Float,size size: CGSize) -> SKPhysicsBody`: This initializer is very similar to the previous one and was also introduced in iOS 8, except that it takes one more argument, `alpha`, as parameter. We can define what should be the alpha value below which the pixels will be ignored, in order to create the new physics body. The rest of the process is the same as the previous one.

After this, let's have a look at how to create an edge-based physics body.

The initialization of edge-based physics bodies

Following is the list of initializers used to make an edge-based physics body:

- `init (edgeLoopFromRect rect: CGRect) -> SKPhysicsBody`: This initializer takes a rectangle as a parameter and returns a new rectangular edge-based physics body.

- `init (edgeFromPoint p1: CGPoint, toPoint p2: CGPoint) -> SKPhysicsBody`: This initializer takes two points as parameters and returns an edge-based physics body between those two points.

- `init (edgeLoopFromPath path: CGPath!) -> SKPhysicsBody`: This initializer takes a `path` as a parameter and returns an edge-based physics body based on that path. The path must not intersect itself. If the path is not closed, it creates a loop by joining the first and the last point of that path automatically.

- `init (edgeChainFromPath path: CGPath!) -> SKPhysicsBody`: This initializer takes a `path` as a parameter and returns an edge chain-based physics body based on that path. The path must not intersect itself.

These are the initialization processes for the physics body—both for volume-based and edge-based ones. We can customize a physics body's behavior by tweaking some of its properties.

The behavior controller properties of a physics body

Following is the list of properties from which we can control the behavior of a physics body:

- `affectedByGravity`: This is a Boolean value. It determines if a physics body will be affected by gravity in the scene. Edge-based physics bodies simply ignore this property as they are not affected by gravity. The default value is `true`.

- `allowsRotation`: This is also a Boolean value. It determines if a physics body will be affected by angular forces and impulses applied to it in the scene. An edge-based physics body simply ignores this property. The default value is `true`.

- `dynamic`: This is a Boolean value too. It determines if a physics body will be moved by the physics simulation in the scene. Edge-based physics bodies simply ignore this property. The default value is `true`.

These are the behavior controller properties for a volume-based physics body. Along with this, a physics body has some of its own physical properties too.

The physical properties of a physics body

These are the properties possessed by a physics body. As you know, the velocity, force, gravity, collision, and so on, depend upon the mass, density, area, and so on, of a body.

Following is the list of physical properties of a physics body.

- `mass`: It is the mass of the body in kilograms.

- `density`: It is the density of the body in kilograms per square meter. The density and mass properties are interrelated. One property is recalculated every time the other is changed. The default value is 1.0.

- `area`: It is the area covered by the body. This is a read-only property and is used to define the mass of the physics body with the help of the `density` property.

- `friction`: It is used to determine how much friction force should be applied to the other physics body in contact with the current body. This property has a value between 0.0 and 1.0. The default value is 0.2.

- `restitution`: It is used to determine the bounciness of the physics body. This property has a value between 0.0 and 1.0. The default value is 0.2.

- `linearDamping`: It is used to reduce the linear velocity of a physics body. This property has a value between 0.0 and 1.0. The default value is 0.1.

- `angularDamping`: It is used to reduce the angular velocity of a physics body. This property has a value between 0.0 and 1.0. The default value is 0.1.

These properties define the physical behavior of a physics body.

The `SKPhysicsBody` class provides some properties and functions for collision control.

Collision control properties and functions

Physics bodies use some category for collision detection with other physics bodies. Collision is very important in almost every game. When objects collide, there is a change in the velocity and discretion of the object, which needs precise calculation of the change in the physical parameters. We have to specify the category of the physics bodies in our game. There is a limitation as we can only define 32 different kinds of categories for the physics bodies in our game. We use these categories to define whether a physics body should collide with another physics body or not. This is very useful behavior and is used in a physics game in Sprite Kit.

Following is the list of collision control properties:

- `categoryBitMask`: This is a mask which defines the category of the physics body. We can have up to 32 different categories. With the help of a category bitmask, you can define which physics bodies should interact with each other. This property is used along with `contactTestBitMark`.

- `collisionBitMask`: This property is used to define the categories of physics bodies which could collide. It is used to determine whether a collision occurs using an AND operation with the other physics body. If the result is a nonzero value, this body will be affected by the collision, otherwise not. This helps you skip collision calculations in case of a minute velocity change.

- `usesPreciseCollisionDetection: Bool`: If `true`, this body will be affected by the collision, otherwise it will pass through the other body in a single frame. A `true` value on either of the bodies will lead to a collision, which means that more computation power will be used by Sprite Kit to detect collisions and perform precise calculations. For very small and fast moving objects, this property can be set to `true`, otherwise the default value is `false`.

- `contactTestBitMask`: This property defines which category a `BitMask` physics body should notify the intersection with the receiving physics body through an AND gate operation. If the value is non-zero, the `SKPhysicsContact` object is created and passed to the physics world delegate.

- `allContactedBodies() -> [AnyObject]`: This is the function which is used to determine if one or more bodies is in contact with the receiving physics body. It simply returns an array of all physics body objects that are in contact with the receiving physics body, that is, the body on which this function is applied.

These collision control properties and functions determine the behavior of two or more physics body collisions or contacts in a physics simulation. But sometimes we need to give velocity or force to a physics body for some specific behavior. The `SKPhysicsBody` class defines some functions which are used to apply force and impulse on physics bodies for this purpose.

Forces and impulses

To move a space ship or a car, we need to apply force in the direction of motion; to keep it moving one has to apply force continuously. Impulse is to change the momentum of an object, for example, to fire a bullet, we need not apply any force once it starts moving.

Following is the list of functions that are used to apply force and impulse on a physics body:

- `func applyForce(_ force: CGVector)`: This function is used to apply a force on the receiving physics body. It takes `force` as a parameter and accelerates the receiving physics body without any angular acceleration.

- `func applyTorque(_ torque: CGFloat)`: This function is used to apply an angular force on the receiving physics body. It takes `torque` as a parameter and applies angular acceleration to the receiving physics body. It does not apply any linear acceleration on the receiving physics body.

- `func applyForce(_ force: CGVector,atPoint point: CGPoint)`: This function is used to apply a force on the receiving physics body at a specific point. As it is applied on a specific point on the physics body, it could change both the angular and linear acceleration of the body.

- `func applyImpulse(_ impulse: CGVector)`: This function is used to apply an impulse to the center of gravity of the receiving physics body. It takes `impulse` as a parameter and affects linear velocity, without changing angular velocity.

- `func applyImpulse(_ impulse: CGVector,atPoint point: CGPoint)`: This function is used to apply an impulse on the receiving physics body at the specific point. As it is applied on a specific point on the physics body, it could change both angular and linear velocity of the receiving physics body.

- `func applyAngularImpulse(_ impulse: CGFloat)`: This function is used to apply an angular impulse on the receiving physics body. It takes `impulse` as a parameter and applies angular velocity on the receiving physics body. It does not apply any linear velocity on the receiving physics body.

Along with these functions, we also need to know the resultant velocity and angular velocity of the physics body. For this purpose, the `SKPhysicsBody` class has some properties.

The velocity of a physics body

Following is the list of functions which are used to apply velocity on a physics body:

- `velocity`: It is used to determine the linear velocity of the physics body.
- `angularVelocity`: It is used to determine the angular velocity of the physics body.
- `resting`: It determines if the physics object is at rest in the physics world. This means that it is not taking part in physics simulation, until awakened by a force or collision. This property helps reduce the calculation in physics simulation, and thus, improves the performance.
- `SKPhysicsBody`: It provides us with some other important properties. Other property `joints`, this property holds an array of `SKPhysicsJoint` objects, which are connected to the receiving physics body.
- `fieldBitMask`: This property is applied on the physics body. Once this body is inside of an `SKFieldNode` object, the `fieldBitMask` property will perform a logical AND operation with the `categoryBitMask` property of the field node. The field node's effect will be applied to this body in case of a nonzero value.
- `charge`: It is used to calculate the electromagnetic field force of an `SKFieldNode` object on the receiver's physics body.
- `pinned`: It determines whether the receiver will be fixed in position with respect to its parent or not. Its default value is `false`. If it is `true`, then the node can freely rotate around its position with respect to its parent, applying physics to our *Platformer* game.

Now, we are going to continue with our *Platformer* game and implement various physics engine capabilities in it. Before we start to apply physics in our game, we need to first make sure that the menu scene that loads initially is `MenuScene` (as discussed in *Chapter 3, Sprites*) and not `NodeMenuScene`. We will be implementing the `NodeMenuScene` class when we discuss about shaders and particle emitters.

Please go over to the `GameViewController.swift` file and in the `GameViewController` class, comment out the following:

```
let menuscene = NodeMenuScene()
```

Instead, write this:

```
let menuscene = MenuScene(size: view.bounds.size, playbutton: "Play",
background:"BG")
```

The above code will make your game load the `MenuScene` class. Now, head over to the `GameScene.swift` file to add physics bodies in our game.

Using GameScene.swift to add physics bodies

Start by opening your `GameScene.swift` file.

1. Edit the `GameScene` class declaration to add `SKPhysicsContactSelegate` as the following:

   ```
   class GameScene: SKScene, SKPhysicsContactDelegate
   ```

2. Then add the following code in it:

   ```swift
   let backgroundNode = SKSpriteNode(imageNamed: "BG")
       var spriteWithoutTexture : SKSpriteNode?
       let myAtlas = SKTextureAtlas(named: "idle.atlas")
       var player:SKSpriteNode =
       SKSpriteNode(imageNamed:"bro5_idle0001@2x")
       var currentno = 0

       // SETTING UP "RUNNING BAR", "BLOCK 1", "Block 2
       let runningBar = SKSpriteNode(imageNamed:"bar")
       let block1 = SKSpriteNode(imageNamed:"block1")
       let block2 = SKSpriteNode(imageNamed:"block2")
       var origRunningBarPositionX = CGFloat(0)
       var maxBarX = CGFloat(0)
       var groundSpeed = 5
       var playerBaseline = CGFloat(0)
       var onGround = true

       // INITIALIZING PHYSICAL PROPERTIES VALUES
       var velocityY = CGFloat(0)
       let gravity = CGFloat(0.6)
       var blockMaxX = CGFloat(0)
       var origBlockPositionX = CGFloat(0)
       var blockStatuses:Dictionary<String,BlockStatus> = [:]

       //COLLISION TYPE BETWEEN "BLOCKS" AND "PLAYER"
       enum ColliderType:UInt32
       {
           case player = 1
           case Block = 2
       }
   ```

If you have a look at the preceding code, you will see that we have added three new images: one is running the bar on top, which our player will run or appear to run, the other two are `block1` and `block2`. These two images are obstacles, with which our player will collide. Apart from this, we have also initialized some physical property values such as velocity, gravity, and so on. We also have defined an enum to control the collision type between `Blocks` and `Player`.

3. Now, add this function to start the execution flow, and to define the contact delegate to detect touch/contact on the screen (touch will help us determine the jump intensity):

```
override func didMoveToView(view: SKView)
{
    self.physicsWorld.contactDelegate = self

    //#1
    addBackGround()
    addRunningBar()
    addPlayer()
    addBlocks()

}
```

In the preceding code, the #1 code block is used for adding the background, running bar, player, and blocks into the scene with the methods. And also for setting up the physics properties, such as `categoryBitMask`, `ContactTestBitMask`, `CollisionBitMask`, and so on.

4. Now, add the following function to generate blocks randomly, taking a number between `50` and `200`; this is used to randomly display blocks on the screen:

```
func random() -> UInt32
    {
        var range = UInt32(50)..<UInt32(200)
        return range.startIndex + arc4random_uniform(range.
endIndex - range.startIndex + 1)
//CREATING BLOCKS FROM LIBRARY METHOD OF iOS
    }
```

5. Now, add the next function for using sprite without texture:

```
func addSpriteWithoutTexture()
    {
        spriteWithoutTexture = SKSpriteNode(texture: nil,
        color:UIColor.redColor(), size: CGSizeMake(100, 100))
```

```
        addChild(spriteWithoutTexture!)
    }
```

6. Add the next function to insert the background in the scene:

```
func addBackGround()
    {
        backgroundNode.zPosition = 0
        var scaleX =
        self.size.width/backgroundNode.size.width
        var scaleY =
        self.size.height/backgroundNode.size.height
        backgroundNode.xScale = scaleX
        backgroundNode.yScale = scaleY
        addChild(backgroundNode)
    }
```

7. Add the following function to define the physics property for the player/character in our game:

```
func addPlayer()
    {

        player.zPosition = 2;
        player.name = "Player"

        // PHYSICS PROPERTIES FOR player
        self.playerBaseline = self.runningBar.position.y +
        (self.runningBar.size.height / 2) +
        (self.player.size.height / 2)
        self.player.position =
        CGPointMake(CGRectGetMinX(self.frame) +
    self.player.size.width + (self.player.size.width / 4),
    self.playerBaseline)
        self.player.physicsBody =
        SKPhysicsBody(circleOfRadius:
        CGFloat(self.player.size.width / 2))
        self.player.physicsBody?.affectedByGravity = false
        self.player.physicsBody?.categoryBitMask =
        ColliderType.player.rawValue
// Will become '1' because its defined in "ColliderType"
enum
        self.player.physicsBody?.contactTestBitMask =
        ColliderType.Block.rawValue
        self.player.physicsBody?.collisionBitMask =
        ColliderType.Block.rawValue

        self.addChild(player)
    }
```

8. Now, set up the running bar; the bar on which the player will appear to run:

```
func addRunningBar()
    {
        self.runningBar.anchorPoint = CGPointMake(0, 0.5)
        self.runningBar.position =
CGPointMake(CGRectGetMinX(self.frame),CGRectGetMinY
(self.frame) + (self.runningBar.size.height / 2))
        self.origRunningBarPositionX =
        self.runningBar.position.x
        self.maxBarX = self.runningBar.size.width -
        self.frame.size.width
        self.maxBarX *= -1
        self.addChild(self.runningBar)
    }
```

9. Time to insert the following function to add the blocks in the game:

```
func addBlocks()
    {
        // PHYSICS PROPERTIES FOR BLOCK 1
        self.block1.position =
        CGPointMake(CGRectGetMaxX(self.frame) +
        self.block1.size.width, self.playerBaseline)
        self.block2.position =
        CGPointMake(CGRectGetMaxX(self.frame) +
        self.block2.size.width, self.playerBaseline +
        (self.block1.size.height / 2))
        self.block1.physicsBody =
        SKPhysicsBody(rectangleOfSize: self.block1.size)
        self.block1.physicsBody?.dynamic = false
        self.block1.physicsBody?.categoryBitMask =
        ColliderType.Block.rawValue
        self.block1.physicsBody?.contactTestBitMask =
        ColliderType.player.rawValue
        self.block1.physicsBody?.collisionBitMask =
        ColliderType.player.rawValue


        // PHYSICS PROPERTIES FOR BLOCK 2
        self.block2.physicsBody =
        SKPhysicsBody(rectangleOfSize: self.block1.size)
        self.block2.physicsBody?.dynamic = false
        self.block2.physicsBody?.categoryBitMask =
        ColliderType.Block.rawValue
        self.block2.physicsBody?.contactTestBitMask =
        ColliderType.player.rawValue
```

```
        self.block2.physicsBody?.collisionBitMask =
        ColliderType.player.rawValue

        self.origBlockPositionX = self.block1.position.x
//ORIGINAL BLOCK POSITION (0,0)
        self.block1.name = "block1"    // SETTING BLOCK
        NAMES
        self.block2.name = "block2"

        // ADDING BLOCK 1 and BLOCK 2 to DICTIONARY
        BLOCKSTATUS
        blockStatuses["block1"] = BlockStatus(isRunning:
false, timeGapForNextRun: random(), currentInterval:
UInt32(0))
        blockStatuses["block2"] = BlockStatus(isRunning:
false, timeGapForNextRun: random(), currentInterval:
UInt32(0))

        self.blockMaxX = 0 - self.block1.size.width / 2

        self.addChild(self.block1)
        self.addChild(self.block2)
    }
```

10. Add the following function, which is called when the user touches the screen. It leads the character to jump:

```
override func touchesBegan(touches: NSSet, withEvent event:
UIEvent) {
        for touch: AnyObject in touches
        {
            let location = touch.locationInNode(self)
            let node = self.nodeAtPoint(location)
            if node.name == player.name
            {
                currentno++
                //changeSpriteFromTextureAtlas()

                if self.onGround
                {
                        self.velocityY = -18.0
                        self.onGround = false
                }
            }
        }
    }
```

11. Also add the next function, which is called when the screen touch is released. It will bring down the character after the jump:

```
override func touchesEnded(touches: NSSet, withEvent event:
UIEvent)
    {
        if self.velocityY < -9.0      //SETTING VELOCITY FOR
        JUMP ACTION IS FINISHED
        {
            self.velocityY = -9.0
        }
    }
```

12. Add the next method to define actions to perform scene-specific updates that need to occur before the scene's actions are evaluated:

```
override func update(currentTime: NSTimeInterval)
    {
        if self.runningBar.position.x <= maxBarX
        {
                self.runningBar.position.x =
                self.origRunningBarPositionX
        }

        // JUMP ACTION
        self.velocityY += self.gravity
        self.player.position.y -= velocityY
        if self.player.position.y < self.playerBaseline
// STOPPING PLAYER TO FALLDOWN FROM BASELINE
        {
            self.player.position.y =
            self.playerBaseline
            velocityY = 0.0
            self.onGround = true
        }
        //move the ground
        runningBar.position.x -=
        CGFloat(self.groundSpeed)
        blockRunner()

    }
```

13. Finally, add the following function to make the blocks run:

```
func blockRunner()
    {
        // LOOP FOR THE DICTIONARY TO GET BLOCKS
        for(block, blockStatus) in self.blockStatuses
        {
            var thisBlock = self.childNodeWithName(block)!
            if blockStatus.shouldRunBlock()
            {
                blockStatus.timeGapForNextRun = random()
                blockStatus.currentInterval = 0
                blockStatus.isRunning = true
            }

            if blockStatus.isRunning
            {

                if thisBlock.position.x > blockMaxX
// IF IT IS POSITIVE (KEEP MOVING BLOCKS FROM RIGHT TO
LEFT)
                {
                    thisBlock.position.x -=
                    CGFloat(self.groundSpeed)
                }
                else
// IF ITS TIME TO OFF THE SCREEN ie when BLOCKS should
DISAPPEAR
                {
                    thisBlock.position.x =
                    self.origBlockPositionX
                    //blockStatus.isRunning = false
                }
            }
            else
            {
                blockStatus.currentInterval++
            }
        }
    }
```

14. Also create one more `swift` file by the name of `BlockStatus.swift`, in Xcode. This file contains code to initialize and run the blocks:

```
class BlockStatus               //
{
    var isRunning = false                 //CURRENTLY
    RUNNING ON SCREEN OR NOT
```

```
var timeGapForNextRun = UInt32(0)      // HOW LONG WE
IT SHOULD WAIT FOR NEXT RUN
var currentInterval = UInt32(0)        //TOTAL
INTERVAL WAITED

// INITIALIZING BLOCK STATUS
init(isRunning:Bool, timeGapForNextRun:UInt32,
currentInterval:UInt32) {
    self.isRunning = isRunning
    self.timeGapForNextRun = timeGapForNextRun
    self.currentInterval = currentInterval
}

// RUNNING BLOCKS
func shouldRunBlock() -> Bool
{
    return self.currentInterval >
    self.timeGapForNextRun
}
}
```

15. Now go ahead and run the game; make sure to experiment with various
    values to discover the behavior of your game. This will increase your
    understanding of physics in Sprite Kit.

And following is the second image:

The preceding two screenshots display the character as static and blocks as moving. We can also perform jumps by touching on the character on the screen:

Did you notice that the player is not running, but instead, the bar under the player and the blocks colliding with it are moving. The character just appears to be running; in this case, we have just implemented the velocity method of jumping, instead of applying force in the y-direction.

Summary

In this chapter, we discussed the physics engine. We learned about `SKPhysicsBody`. Now we know very well about edge-based and volume-based physics bodies in Sprite Kit. In our game, blocks coming towards the character are volume-based bodies. We also learned about the various initialization methods for these kinds of physics bodies. We learned how to apply the physics engine of Sprite Kit in a game, so as to explore its features.

In the next chapter, we will learn about animating sprites in Sprite Kit and adding various types of controls in our game. Also, we will discuss about collisions and SceneKit integration through Sprite Kit.

6
Animating Sprites, Controls, and SceneKit

In the previous chapter, we learned about physics engine in detail. We discussed `SKPhysicsBody`, that is, edge-based and volume-based physics bodies. We also got to know about the various initialization methods and physics properties, which helped us in integrating physics into our *Platformer* game. Now we have a much clear idea about how to simulate physics in a Sprite Kit game.

It is always good to have nice animated features in our game to enhance the user experience; this Sprite Kit has the `SKAction` class, which helps us to apply actions on nodes such as moving of nodes, rotating of nodes, scaling of nodes, and so on. For example, using animations during player movement or depicting collisions using animations, and so on. It's time for us to discuss about the `SKAction` class and also about implementing animations in our *Platformer* game.

Along with animation, we are also going to discuss about how we can provide controls in our game, such as having a reaction when the user taps on the screen or using the accelerometer to respond to directions in a game. We will also implement controls in our *Platformer* game and add a jump button to make the player jump over the blocks.

Scene Kit is a 3D graphics framework provided by Apple, we can use SceneKit's 3D elements in our Sprite Kit game to further enhance the gaming experience and have a better gameplay if required. We are going to discuss about how we can integrate SceneKit in a Sprite Kit game.

Animating nodes

Animated pictures give a very dynamic and polished feel during a gameplay; it is always preferred to have animations in our game. To add animations in Sprite Nodes, we can use the SKAction class properties and methods, which add the animations to the Sprite Kit nodes. Let's discuss about the SKAction class in detail.

SKAction

Properties and methods of the SKAction class help in providing the actions to the nodes in a scene. Actions are used to change the arrangement and appearance of the node to which they are attached. Actions in a node are executed when the scene runs its nodes.

To assign an action we can call the particular SKAction class method as required. Then, we can configure the properties of the actions. In the end, for the execution of the action, we call the node object's runAction() method and pass the action's object.

Adding a single action to a node

There are two steps to add a single action to the node:

1. **Creating an action**: First of all, we create an action which can perform a particular activity such as rotating, scaling, moving, and so on, on the Sprite Kit node.

2. **Executing an action**: Finally, we run the action on the node by calling the runAction() method on that node.

Adding multiple actions to a node

There are three steps involved in the process of adding multiple actions to the node:

1. **Creating actions**: Here, instead of creating a single action, we can create multiple actions to perform different behaviors on the Sprite Kit node.

2. **Creating action sequence**: Here, we are going to create the order of execution in which the actions should behave in the Sprite Kit node.

3. **Executing the action**: Finally, we are going to run the action by specifying the action sequence in the runAction() method on the node.

Creating actions

There are various types of actions which can be applied on a node to make it behave differently, now we are going to study about most of them in detail.

Moving nodes using actions

The SKAction class provides various action methods for moving nodes on a scene. They are as follows:

- func moveByX(x: CGFloat, y : CGFloat, duration sec: NSTimeInterval): This will move the node to its new position. Here, Delta of x, Delta of y, and duration in seconds are passed as parameters.

- func moveBy(delta: CGVector, duration sec: NSTimeInterval): This will move the node relative to its current position. Here, Delta vector pointing to a new position and duration in seconds are passed as parameters.

- moveTo(location: CGPoint, duration sec: NSTimeInterval): This will move the node to a new position. Location of the new position and duration in seconds are passed as parameters. Here location is a CGpoint value whose default value is (0,0).

- func moveToX(x: CGFloat, duration sec: NSTimeInterval): This will move the node horizontally. In this, the x value and the duration of the action are passed as parameters.

- func moveToY(y: CGFloat, duration sec: NSTimeInterval): This will move the node vertically along a relative path. In this, the y value and the duration of the action in seconds are passed as parameters.

- func followPath(path: CGPath, duration sec: NSTimeInterval): This will move the node along a relative path. path and sec are taken as parameters, in which path is a CGpath value which is relative to the current position of the node.

- func followPath(path: CGPath, speed: CGFloat): This will move the node along a relative path at a specified speed. The unit of speed is points per second.

- func followPath(path: CGPath, asOffset : Bool, orientToPath : Bool, duration : NSTimeInterval): This function will move the node along the path. In this function, we pass four parameters: one is the path on which the node will move; the second is the offset parameter, which is either true or false. true represents that the points in the path are relative offsets to the initial position of the node, and on the other hand false represents that the points are absolute in nature. orientToPath will be a Boolean property if the true node can follow the path along the z axis.

- `func followPath( path: CGPath, asOffset : Bool, orientToPath : Bool, speed : CGFloat)`: This function will move the node along the path at a specified speed.

Rotating nodes using actions

The `SKAction` class provides various action methods for rotating nodes on a scene. They are:

- `func rotateByAngle( radians: CGFloat, duration sec: NSTimeInterval)`: This functions helps in rotating the node at a specified angle. It takes two parameters: one is the amount in which the node is to be rotated in `radians`, and the other is the duration of the rotation in `seconds`. This rotation is relative to the node.

- `func rotateToAngle( radians: CGFloat, duration sec: NSTimeInterval)`: This function helps in rotating the node to an absolute angle, in the counterclockwise direction. It also takes two parameters: one is the angle to rotate the node, which is measured in `radians`, and the other is the duration of the animation in seconds.

- `func rotateToAngle(radians: CGFloat, duration sec: NSTimeInterval, shortestUnitArc shortestUnitArc: Bool)`: This function helps in rotating the node to an absolute angle. It takes three parameters: one is the angle to which the node is to be rotated, the second is the duration in seconds, and the third is a Boolean value to assign whether we want the smallest rotation path or not. If `true`, then the rotation will be in the shortest direction, otherwise the rotation will be interpolated within the discrete points.

Changing the animation speed of a node

The `SKAction` class provides various action methods for changing a node's animation speed. They are as follows:

- `func speedBy( speed: CGFloat, duration sec: NSTimeInterval)`: With this function, we can control the speed of a node's actions. It takes two parameters: one is the amount of `speed` to be added in the node, and the other is the `duration` of the animation in seconds.

- `func speedTo(speed: CGFloat, duration sec: NSTimeInterval)`: With this function too, we can control the speed of the node's actions. But instead of passing the parameter that adds its value to the previous speed, this function changes the `speed` to the set value. The other parameter passed is the `duration` of animation in seconds.

Changing the scale position of a node

The SKAction class provides various action methods for scaling a node. They are as follows:

- func scaleBy(scale: CGFloat, duration sec: NSTimeInterval): With this function, you can change the xScale and yScale values of a node. This function takes two parameters: one is the amount to be added in the x and y values of the node, and the other is the duration of the animation. This scaling applies to the current size.

- func scaleTo(scale: CGFloat, duration sec: NSTimeInterval): With this function too, you can change the x and y values of a node. It takes two parameters: one is the new value of the node's x and y values, and the other is the duration of the animation.

- func scaleXBy (xScale: CGFloat, y yScale: CGFloat, duration sec: NSTimeInterval): With this function, you can change the x and y values of the node. Three parameters are passed in this function: first is the amount to be added in the node's x value, second is the amount to be added in the node's y value, and the third is the duration of the animation. This function is used when you have to scale the x and y of a node with different values.

- func scaleXTo(xScale: CGFloat, y yScale: CGFloat, duration sec: NSTimeInterval): With this function too, you can change the x and y values of the node differently. But instead of passing the value to add in the x and y, you can set the x and y scale to new values by passing the respective parameters.

- func scaleXTo(scale: CGFloat, duration sec: NSTimeInterval): With this function, you can only change the x value of a node to a new value. It takes two parameters: one is the node's x value and the other is the duration of the animation.

- func scaleYTo(scale: CGFloat, duration sec: NSTimeInterval): With this function, you can only change the y value of a node to a new value. It takes two parameters: one is the node's y value and the other is the duration of the animation.

Showing or hiding a node

The SKAction class provides various action methods for hiding or showing a node on a scene. Let's have a look at both of these functions:

- func unhide(): With this function, you can create an action to make a node visible. This function was introduced in iOS 8.0.

- `func hide()`: With this function, you can create an action to make a node hidden. This function was introduced in iOS 8.0 as well.

Changing the transparency of a node

With the help of `SKAction`, you can also change the transparency of a node. The following functions help you achieve this:

- `func fadeInWithDuration( sec: NSTimeInterval)`: You can change the alpha value of a node to `1.0` with this function. Only one parameter is passed with this function, which is the duration of the animation.

- `func fadeOutWithDuration( sec: NSTimeInterval)`: You can change the alpha value of a node to `0.0` with this function. Only one parameter is passed with this function, which is the duration of the animation.

- `func fadeAlphaBy( factor: CGFloat, duration sec: NSTimeInterval)`: With this function, you can control the amount of alpha value to be added to the node. You pass two parameters in this function: one is the amount to be added to the alpha value of the node, and the other is the `duration` of the node.

- `func fadeAlphaTo(alpha: CGFloat, duration sec: NSTimeInterval)`: With this function, you can set a new alpha value for the node. Two parameters are passed in this function: one is the node's new alpha value and the other is the `duration` of the node.

Changing the content of a sprite node

With some `SKAction` functions, you can create actions to change the content of a sprite node. Let's have a look at them:

- `func resizeByWidth( width: CGFloat, height: CGFloat, duration: NSTimeInterval)`: This function creates an action which adjusts the size of a sprite node. This function takes three parameters: the first is the amount to be added to the sprite's `width`, the second is the amount to be added to the sprite's `height`, and the third is the `duration` of the animation.

- `func resizeToHeight( height: CGFloat, duration: NSTimeInterval)`: This function creates an action that changes the `height` of a sprite to a new value. One parameter passed is the new `height` of the sprite, and the second parameter is the `duration` of the animation.

- `func resizeToWidth(width: CGFloat, duration: NSTimeInterval):` This function creates an action that changes the `width` of a sprite to a new value. One parameter passed is the new `width` of the sprite, and the second parameter is the `duration` of the animation.

- `func resizeToWidth( width: CGFloat, height: CGFloat, duration: NSTimeInterval):` This function creates an action that changes the `width` and `height` of a sprite node to a new value. You can specify the new `height` and `width` separately in this function. It takes three parameters: one is the new `width` of the sprite, the second is the new `height` of the sprite, and the third is the `duration` of the animation.

- `func setTexture(texture: SKTexture):` This function helps in creating an action that changes the sprite's texture. Only one parameter is passed in this function, which is the sprite's new `texture`.

- `func setTexture( texture: SKTexture, resize: Bool):` This function helps in creating an action that changes the sprite's texture. Along with this, you can also control whether the sprite should be resized to match the new texture or not. The two parameters passed are the new `texture` to use on the sprite and the Boolean to control the resizing.

- `func animateWithTextures(textures: [AnyObject], timePerFrame sec: NSTimeInterval):` This function creates an action that animates changes in a sprite's texture. When the action executes, the `texture` property animates the array of the `texture`, which is passed as a parameter. The action continues until all the textures in the array have finished animating. Two parameters are passed in this function: one is the array of `textures`, and the other is the time in which each texture in the array will be displayed.

- `func animateWithTextures( textures: [AnyObject], timePerFrame sec: NSTimeInterval, resize: Bool, restore: Bool):` This function creates an action which animates changes to the sprite's texture and can also resize the sprite to the new texture, if required. It takes four parameters: one is the array of `textures` that are used when animating the sprite, the second is the time in which each texture will be displayed, the third is a Boolean value to control the resizing of the sprite to match the new texture, and the fourth is the restoring of the size of the sprite to the original texture size.

- `func colorizeWithColor(color: UIColor, colorBlendFactor: CGFloat, duration sec: NSTimeInterval):` This function creates an animation that animates a sprite's color and blend factor. Three parameters are passed in this function: one is `color` for the new sprite, the second is the new blend factor, and the third is the `duration` of the animation.

- func colorizeWithColorBlendFactor(colorBlendFactor: CGFloat, duration sec: NSTimeInterval): This function will create an animation that animates the sprite's blend factor. It takes two parameters: one is the new blend factor and the other is the duration of the animation.

Some other important actions

By now, we have discussed most of the important functions that are used to create actions on a node. Now, we are going to have a look at some other important functions used in creating actions on a node in Sprite Kit:

- func runAction(action: SKAction, onChildWithName name: String): This function will create an action that will, in turn, run an action on a node's child. You pass the action to execute and take the name of the child object as parameters.

- func group(actions: [AnyObject]): You can run a collection of actions in parallel, using this function's action. It takes an array of SKAction objects as a parameter.

- func sequence(actions: [AnyObject]): You can run a collection of actions sequentially, using this function's action. It takes an array of SKAction objects as a parameter. The order of actions is the same as the order of actions passed in the array.

- func repeatAction(action: SKAction, count count: Int): You can create an action to repeat an action that is specified to repeat a number of times. The action to repeat and the count of repetitions are passed as parameters.

- func repeatActionForever(action: SKAction): It creates an action that, in turn, repeats another action forever. It takes the action to repeat as a parameter.

- func reversedAction(): With this action, you can reverse the behavior of another action.

Adding controls in Sprite Kit

Adding controls in a Sprite Kit doesn't need any external predefined framework; we can implement the controls in Sprite Kit using the following methods:

- Tapping
- Gesture recognitions (swiping in any direction, pinching, rotating)
- Moving sprites using the accelerometer

Let's discuss each of the preceding controls in detail and also how we can implement them in our game.

Node tapping and clicking

We have four override methods for handling touch events with a `UIResponder` class, which is part of `UIKit` provided by Apple. Let's learn about them:

- `func touchesBegan(touches:Set<NSObject>, withEvent event:UIEvent)`: This method is called whenever a user touches the view/window

- `func touchesMoved(touches:Set<NSObject>, withEvent event:UIEvent)`: This method is called whenever a user moves his finger on the view/window

- `func touchesEnded(touches:Set<NSObject>, withEvent event:UIEvent)`: This method is called whenever a user removes the finger from view/window

- `func touchesCancelled(touches:Set<NSObject>!, withEvent event:UIEvent!)`: This method is called whenever system events, such as low memory warnings and so on, happen

To implement an action when someone taps on a node on the scene, we will first get the tapped location on the scene, and if the tapped location is within the node's co-ordinate axis points, then we can define the actions for that tap. This will be implemented in the `touchesBegan()` method.

Sprite Kit includes a category in `UITouch`; this is one of its best features. `UITouch` comes with two methods, namely, `locationInNode()` and `previousLocationInNode()`. These methods find the coordinates of a touch within an `SKNode` object's coordinate system.

In our game, we will use it to find out where the touch happened within the scene's coordinate system.

Gesture recognitions (swiping in any direction, pinching, or rotating)

If you need to detect gestures in your game, such as taps, pinches, pans, or rotations, it's extremely easy with Swift and the built-in `UIGestureRecognizer` classes.

Following is a code snippet for gesture recognitions in Swift; it will implement swiping left, right, top, and bottom.

First, we set up four functions, one for each direction, to handle whatever we want to do when the user swipes the screen in those directions. Then, in the `didMoveToView` statement, we create the `UISwipeGestureRecognizer` variables for each direction and add them to the view. Notice the `action:` `selector` part of each, calls their respective functions in the following code:

```
func swipedRight(sender:UISwipeGestureRecognizer){
  println("swiped right")
}

func swipedLeft(sender:UISwipeGestureRecognizer){
  println("swiped left")
}

func swipedUp(sender:UISwipeGestureRecognizer){
  println("swiped up")
}

func swipedDown(sender:UISwipeGestureRecognizer){
  println("swiped down")
}

override func didMoveToView(view: SKView) {

  /* Setup your scene here */

  let swipeRight:UISwipeGestureRecognizer =
  UISwipeGestureRecognizer(target: self, action:
  Selector("swipedRight:"))
  swipeRight.direction = .Right
  swipeRight.numberOfTouchesRequired = 1
  view.addGestureRecognizer(swipeRight)

  let swipeLeft:UISwipeGestureRecognizer =
  UISwipeGestureRecognizer(target: self, action:
  Selector("swipedLeft:"))
  swipeLeft.direction = .Left
  swipeRight.numberOfTouchesRequired = 1
  view.addGestureRecognizer(swipeLeft)

  let swipeUp:UISwipeGestureRecognizer =
  UISwipeGestureRecognizer(target: self, action:
  Selector("swipedUp:"))
  swipeUp.direction = .Up
```

```
swipeRight.numberOfTouchesRequired = 1
view.addGestureRecognizer(swipeUp)

let swipeDown:UISwipeGestureRecognizer =
UISwipeGestureRecognizer(target: self, action:
Selector("swipedDown:"))
swipeDown.direction = .Down
swipeRight.numberOfTouchesRequired = 1
view.addGestureRecognizer(swipeDown)
```

Using the preceding code block, you can implement swipe control in a Sprite Kit game. When the user swipes in a particular direction, the UISwipeGestureRecognizer will recognize the direction of the user's swipe and the swipe gesture object will be added to the gesture through the addGestureRecognizer() method. So, the particular object will be sent for the function and the appropriate method will be called, and after that, the respective actions will be executed as desired.

Moving sprites with an accelerometer

An accelerometer is a sensor that measures proper acceleration ("g-force"). Proper acceleration is not the same as coordinate acceleration (rate of change of velocity). A lot of games use an accelerometer as a controller. We can also use it in our Sprite Kit game.

Let's have a look at how we can implement an accelerometer in a Sprite Kit game. We will not be using an accelerometer in our *Platformer* game, but it would be good to have knowledge of the same.

As a primary point, we need to read values from the accelerometer, so we need to import the CoreMotion framework. Add the following line right after the import SpriteKit line:

```
import CoreMotion

add the following properties.

var airplane = SKSpriteNode()
var motionManager = CMMotionManager()
var destX:CGFloat = 0.0
```

The CMMotionManager object is the gateway to the motion services provided by iOS. In the didMoveToView method, the custom code is executed. Let's have a look at it:

```
override func didMoveToView(view: SKView) {
    /* Setup your scene here */
    // 1
    airplane = SKSpriteNode(imageNamed: "Airplane")
    airplane.position = CGPointMake(frame.size.width/2,
    frame.size.height/2)
    self.addChild(airplane)
      if motionManager.accelerometerAvailable == true
{

        // 2motionManager.startAccelerometerUpdatesToQueue
(NSOperationQueue.currentQueue(), withHandler:{
            data, error in
              var currentX = self.airplane.position.x

            // 3
            if data.acceleration.x < 0 {
            self.destX = currentX + CGFloat(data.acceleration.x * 100)
            }
            else if data.acceleration.x > 0 {
            self.destX = currentX + CGFloat(data.acceleration.x * 100)
            }
        })
        }
    }
```

Please refer the comments in the preceding code to the following points:

1. The image will be loaded and centered in the main view.
2. The startAccelerometerUpdatesQueue method reads input from the accelerometer and constantly gets new updates.
3. If the acceleration value is negative, the value is subtracted from the x position, hence the airplane will move left. If the acceleration value is positive, the value will be added to the x position.

   The actual movement will be done on the update method, which will be called at each frame.

   ```
   override func update(currentTime: CFTimeInterval) {
       /* Called before each frame is rendered */
       var action = SKAction.moveToX(destX, duration: 1)
       self.airplane.runAction(action)
   }
   ```

A `moveToX` action is assigned to the airplane. This code will be a helpful reference if you want to implement accelerometer for controlling a game. Now, let's read about SceneKit.

An introduction to SceneKit

SceneKit is a framework that can be used to implement the features of 3D graphic components into our iOS games. SceneKit provides a facility for integrating a high performance rendering engine at a greater level. It also offers a facility for importing, manipulating, and rendering 3D graphic assets.

It is fairly easy in iOS 8, to integrate SceneKit elements in a Sprite Kit game. First of all, you just have to import the SceneKit framework in the required Sprite Kit class. Then, you are all set to access all the methods and properties of SceneKit.

Adding animations and controls in our Platformer game

After discussing about the `SKAction` class and various methods to add controls in our game, it's time to revisit our *Platformer* game and implement some of them.

Adding actions

Now, it's time to add actions in our game. Let's start with adding animation to the player and block collision. Until the last chapter, there was no collision effect between the player and the blocks.

Here we will add collision between the block and the player. Along with this, we can make the player die in an animated way. We can denote the animation after the player and block collision as a player death animation.

First of all, we will update the maximum size of the X-axis for the blocks, because currently, the blocks are being destroyed before the end of the running bar. Hence, we will replace the respective code with an updated one.

Replace `self.blockMaxX = 0 - self.block1.size.width / 2` with `self.blockMaxX = 0 - self.runningBar.size.width` in the `addBlocks()` method, in the `GameScene.swift` file.

Now, we will work on the part where the block and the player collides. For this, we will use a library method function, didBeginContact(), which is called when the collision happens, as we have already set all the required physics properties such as, contactTestBitMask, categoryBitMask, and collisionBitMask for the blocks and the player in the addBlocks() method, in the GameScene.swift file.

Include the didBeginContact() method and add the following code, in which we are defining actions when the player and the block collide:

```
func didBeginContact(contact: SKPhysicsContact)
    {


        var inOutActionWhenPlayerDied = SKAction.scaleBy(0.5,
        duration: 0.5)
        var upActionWhenPlayerDied =
        SKAction.moveToY(self.player.size.height * 4, duration: 2)
        var removeFromParent = SKAction.self.removeFromParent()


    self.player.runAction(SKAction.sequence(
    [inOutActionWhenPlayerDied,
    inOutActionWhenPlayerDied.reversedAction(),
    upActionWhenPlayerDied, removeFromParent]),
    gotoMenuScreen)


    }
```

In the preceding function, we used inOutWhenPlayerDied for scaling a player by multiplying a float value of 0.5 and also specifying the duration as 0.5 seconds. In upActionWhenPlayerDied, we moved the player along the y-axis by multiplying the player's height with a float value 4, with the duration of animation as 2 seconds.

After these animations, we should also remove the player from the scene, and also from the node tree. This is taken care of by removeFromParent.

Next, we call the action in the desired sequence.

If you notice in the preceding function that we just added in our *Platformer* game, when calling the sequence, we have also reversed an action by using reversedAction(). We also call the gotoMenuScreen function in our sequence. Let's discuss about the same:

This is how our game will look after adding this action sequence:

The animation for when the player collides with a block.

Transiting from GameScene to MenuScene

After the player's death, it is time to call the `gotoMenuScreen()` method for transiting to the `MenuScreen`. Add the following function in the `GameScene` class to do the same:

```
func gotoMenuScreen()
    {
        self.player.removeFromParent()

        let transitionEffect =
        SKTransition.doorsCloseHorizontalWithDuration(1.5)
        menuSceneInstance = MenuScene(size: self.size ,
        playbutton: "Play", background: "BG")
        menuSceneInstance!.anchorPoint = CGPoint(x: 0.5, y: 0.5)
        self.view?.presentScene(menuSceneInstance ,
        transition:transitionEffect)

    }
```

A slight glimpse of the transition:

The door close transition after the player's death.

Adding controls in our game

For controlling the player, we can make him jump over the blocks and save him from dying. Currently, this is being done by tapping on the player, but it is better to have a button for this action.

To implement the **JUMP** button in our game, first we need to create a sprite node for the **JUMP** button in the GameScene.swift file. Create a sprite node with the name, btnjump, and then assign the node with an image for the button; we can call the image jump. Add the following code for this feature:

```
var btnJump:SKNode = SKSpriteNode(imageNamed: "jump")
```

Now, we need to position our button on the GameScene. For this, we can add the following code before the addBackground() function call in the didMoveToView() method.

```
self.btnJump.position = CGPointMake(-(self.size.width/2.2),
-(self.size.height/4))
        self.addChild(btnJump)
```

And now your `didMoveToView()` function should look like the following:

```
override func didMoveToView(view: SKView)
{
    self.physicsWorld.contactDelegate = self

    // JUMP BUTTON POSITION SETTING AND ADDING ONTO THE SCREEN
    self.btnJump.position = CGPointMake
    (-(self.size.width/2.2), -(self.size.height/4))
    self.addChild(btnJump)

    addBackGround()
    addRunningBar()
    addPlayer()
    addBlocks()
    //addSpriteWithoutTexture()
}
```

Till now, we have just added the **JUMP** button on scene but we didn't define the action of when the button will be clicked. So, let's write a block of code for performing this action:

```
if self.btnJump.containsPoint(location)
{
    println("tapped!")
    if self.onGround
    {
        self.velocityY = -18.0
        self.onGround = false
    }
}
```

Add the preceding block of code in the `touchesBegan` method of `GameScene.swift`. Now your `touchesBegan()` method function should look like the following:

```
override func touchesBegan(touches: NSSet, withEvent event:
UIEvent) {
    for touch: AnyObject in touches
    {
        let location = touch.locationInNode(self)
        let node = self.nodeAtPoint(location)
        if node.name == player.name
        {
            currentno++
            //changeSpriteFromTextureAtlas()
```

```
            if self.onGround
            {
                    self.velocityY = -18.0
                    self.onGround = false
            }
        }

        // JUMP BUTTON ACTION
        if self.btnJump.containsPoint(location)
        {
            println("tapped!")
            if self.onGround
            {

                self.velocityY = -18.0
                self.onGround = false
            }
        }

    }
}
```

Following is how the GameScene will look after adding the **JUMP** button:

The JUMP button now appears on the screen

Now, if you run the game, there will be two major changes: one is the animation of the player's death during collision with the blocks, and the other is the **JUMP** button to make the player jump over the blocks.

Summary

In this chapter, we learned about the SKAction class in detail; this class is responsible for creating actions for nodes. We also discussed about various types of controls by which a Sprite Kit game can be played (such as, tapping, gesture recognition, and accelerometer). We also read about SceneKit and how we can integrate SceneKit in a Sprite Kit game. Now, our *Platformer* game has two new features. One is the player's death animation and the other is the **JUMP** button to control the player's jump.

In the next chapter, we will learn about the particle system and shaders. Along with this, we will also add particle effects in our *Platformer* game, to enhance gameplay experience.

7
Particle Effects and Shaders

In the previous chapter, we discussed in detail how to animate nodes, controls, the SceneKit method, and so on. We also discussed handling scene animations. We learned the SKAction class properties and methods along with learning about various controls by which a game can be played, such as gesture recognition or accelerometer.

We added player animations, controls, and actions in our *Platformer* game, this has made the game pretty fun to play and interesting to learn.

In this chapter, we will study particle effects and shaders in a Sprit Kit game. Particle effect is a very exciting ability provided by Sprite Kit. We can generate particles using the SKEmitterNode object; these particles create beautiful visual effects such as rain, fire, bokeh, spark, and so on. Shaders were introduced in Sprite Kit with iOS 8. Shaders are used to give customized special effects to scenes. The SKShader class is used to include shaders in our Sprite Kit game.

Particle effects

Particle effects in games is a technique in which small sprites or other graphical objects are used to simulate a diffused effect, for example, rendering of the following effects by the particle system is very common:

- Fire
- Explosion
- Smoke
- Moving water
- Falling leaves
- Clouds

- Fog
- Snow
- Dust
- Meteors
- Stars
- Galaxies
- Trails

The entire behavior in particle effect is defined by the emitter node. A particle in Sprite Kit is similar to a SKSpriteNode object where it renders a textured or non-textured image that can be sized, colorized, or blended in the scene.

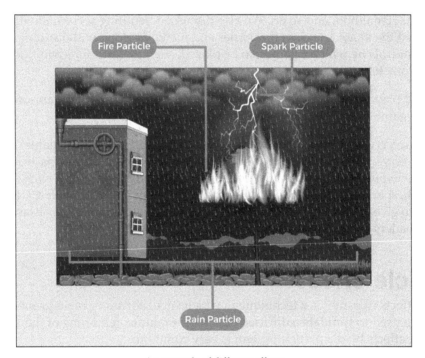

An example of different effects

The SKEmitter node

The SKEmitterNode object is a node that automatically creates and renders small sprites. We can configure the emitter node properties from our Xcode itself. We use the particle emitter editor for this purpose.

We can use target nodes to change the destination of particles. Here is a sample code snippet to demonstrate how we can implement the same.

```
// CREATING THE EMITTER NODE
var emitter:SKEmitterNode = (fileNamed: "PlayerCollide.sks")
// SETTING THE EMITTER POSITION AND NAME
emitter.position = CGPointMake(0,-40)
emitter.name = "playerCollide"
// SEND THE PARTICLES TO THE SCENE
emitter.targetNode = self.scene
// ADDING EMITTER NODE
self.addChild(emitter)
```

Let's discuss the properties and methods that are used while implementing Sprite Kit's emitter node.

Creating the particle effect

Sprite Kit provides properties and variables to customize particle effects as per their requirement in a game. Let's discuss these properties and variables:

- `var particleBirthRate`: In this property, you define the number of particles created by the emitter every second. The default value of this is `0.0`.

- `func advanceSimulationTime( sec:NSTimeInterval )`: This method helps you advance the emitter particle simulation. It takes time in seconds as its parameter, which is the time required to simulate. Preferably, this method is used to preoccupy an emitter node with particles after its addition to scene.

- `var numParticlesToEmit`: In this property, you define the number of particles the emitter has to emit. By default, its value is `0`, which means that the emitter creates infinite particles.

- `func resetSimulation ()`: This method removes all the particles and restarts the simulation. Resetting the simulation clears its internal state.

- `var targetNode`: As discussed earlier, we can use `targetNode` to change the destination of the particles. If the property is `nil`, then the particles are treated to be children of the emitter node. When this property points to the target node, then new particles are treated as if they are children of the target node, but the previously generated particles are calculated based on the emitter node's properties. Its default value is nil.

Properties for determining a particle's lifetime

This is the time for which the user-created particle will stay alive and functional. When the lifetime drains out and drops below zero, the particle will be killed.

- `var particleLifetime`: This property determines the average lifetime of a particle in seconds. Its default value is `0.0`.

- `var particleLifetimeRange`: We specify a range in this property, the lifetime of a particle is determined randomly within this range.

It's now time to add a particle effect in our *Platformer* game.

Adding the particle effect in our Platformer game

Let's integrate particle effect at player collision in our *Platformer* game. We will make a particle simulation at the time of collision between blocks and the player.

As an initial step for implementation, lets create a particle effect. Go to the **Project Navigator** and add new **File** | **SpriteKit Particle File** | **Spark** | **Create**.

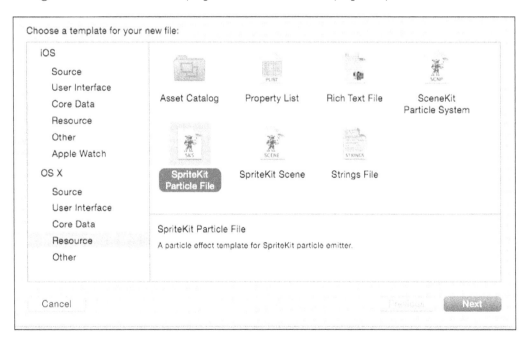

You can choose from a list of particle templates, such as **Snow**, **Bokeh**, **Fire**, **Rain**, **Spark**, and so on. Here we are using the **Spark** effect template:

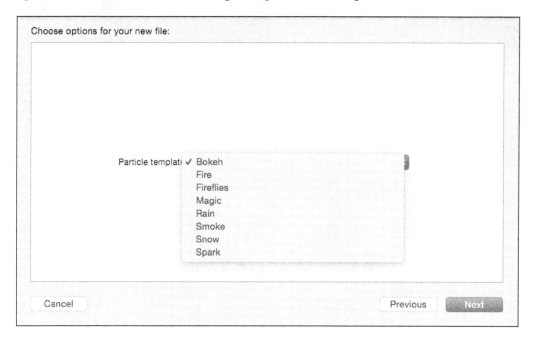

Open the `ParticleEffectPlayerCollide.sks` file we just created. Particle effect files are saved with the extension, `.sks`. You can change the different properties of selected particle effects using the particle emitter editor, which you can access on the right-hand side.

The particle emitter editor in Sprite Kit

Let's discuss some of the properties, which are displayed on the **SpriteKit Particle Emitter** panel:

- **Particle Texture**: You can select an image to be used for creating the particle. For particle texture, images related to the project can also be used. To assign the image, one must keep in mind that a complex and larger image will require excessive use of resources. A simple and small image is advisable.

- **Birthrate**: This property is used to set the rate at which the emitter generates the particles. If the birthrate is more than the particle effect, it will look more intensive. So, it's always recommended to follow the lower birthrate for an optimum frame rate.

- **Lifetime**: This property will define the total lifetime of the particle on the screen. Here, **Range** refers to the random value from the first value **+** or **-** range.

- **Position Range**: This property will tell you how far from the origin emitter node the effect should be, using **X** and **Y** co-ordinate values. Change in this property affects the size of the emitter.

- **Angle**: This property will tell the angle in which the particle effect should happen. This will also use the **Start** and **Range** values.

- **Speed**: This property will define the initial speed at which the effect should happen. This will also use the **Start** and **Range** values.

- **Acceleration**: This property will take care of the acceleration at which the particles should appear from the source emitter using **X** and **Y** coordinates.

- **Alpha**: This property will take care of the transparency of the effect. This will also use the **Start** and **Range** values with a **Speed**.

- **Scale**: This property will define the **Scale** position for the texture/image that is used for the effect. This will also use the **Start**, **Range**, and **Speed** values.

- **Rotation**: This property is used to define the **Rotation** speed for the particle effect. This will also use the **Start**, **Range**, and **Speed** values.

- The **Color Blend** factor: This property is used to define the color that is used in the particle effect lifetime. Where the particles may follow different colors in their particle lifetime. This will use the **Factor**, **Range**, and **Speed** values for defining the property.

Adding the code to facilitate the particle effect

Once you are done with setting up the desired properties, create a particle node object (the SKEmitterNode object) in the GameScene.swift file:

```
var particlePlayerNode = SKEmitterNode(fileNamed:
"ParticleEffectPlayerCollide.sks")
```

Now, set the position in the didMoveToView() method and also hide the particle node that is created. Finally, add the particle node into the player. Now the didMoveToView() method should look like the following code:

```
override func didMoveToView(view: SKView)
    {
        self.physicsWorld.contactDelegate = self
        // JUMP BUTTON POSITION SETTING AND ADDING ONTO THE
        SCREEN
        self.btnJump.position = CGPointMake
(-(self.size.width/2.2), -(self.size.height/4))
        self.addChild(btnJump)

  //PROPERTIES FOR PARTICLE NODE        CHAPTER 7
        self.particlePlayerNode.zPosition = 1
        self.particlePlayerNode.hidden = true

        addBackGround()
        addRunningBar()
        addPlayer()

        //ADDING PARTICLE NODE ON SCREEN (AS CHILD TO PLAYER)
        self.player.addChild(self.particlePlayerNode)

        addBlocks()
        //addSpriteWithoutTexture()
    }
```

Now, let's define when this particle effect should happen, un-hiding the particlePlayerNode we created within the didBeginContact() method, as this method will be called whenever the collision happens.

The `didBeginContact` method should look as follows:

```
func didBeginContact(contact: SKPhysicsContact)
{
    // SHOWING PARTICLE EFFECT WHEN COLLISION HAPPENS
    self.particlePlayerNode.hidden = false

    var inOutActionWhenPlayerDied = SKAction.scaleBy(0.5,
    duration: 0.5)
    var upActionWhenPlayerDied =
    SKAction.moveToY(self.player.size.height * 4, duration: 2)
    var removeFromParent = SKAction.self.removeFromParent()
```

```
self.player.runAction(SKAction.sequence
([inOutActionWhenPlayerDied,
inOutActionWhenPlayerDied.reversedAction(),
upActionWhenPlayerDied, removeFromParent]),
gotoMenuScreen)
```

```
}
```

This is how the collision will look with the particle effect:

Now, we have successfully added the particle effect in our *Platformer* game, and it's time to discuss about shaders and how we can add them in our game.

Shaders

Shaders in Sprite Kit facilitate SKScenenode to appear with a special, customized, drawing behavior. This can be achieved by creating the SKShader objects and assigning a custom OpenGL ES fragment shader.

If a custom shader (the SKShader object) needs to provide a uniform shader, then you need to create one or more SKUniform objects and associate them with your shader objects. Shader programs are primarily divided into:

- Vertex shaders
- Fragment shaders

Let's discuss about both of these in detail:

- **Vertex shaders**: These shaders work on each vertex and most of the calculation is done on the vertex part. They are set by Sprite Kit automatically. As the computation of these shaders are mostly done on the vertex part, not much of the CPU's resources are consumed in the formation.

- **Fragment shaders**: These shaders are written in OpenGL Shading Language. As the name suggests, they work on each pixel. They use very heavy computation and hence are avoided when too many shaders are required.

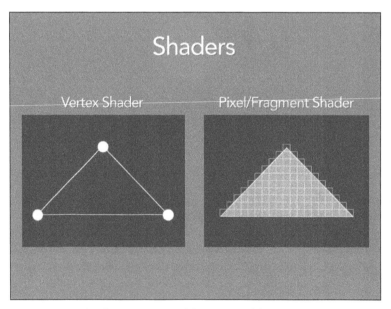

A graphical representation of the vertex and fragment shaders

A fact about using custom shaders

Writing your own shaders is a complicated task if you have not done GLSL code before, but it makes sense to add shader scripts to an existing Sprite Kit.

You can easily procure shader files online from various websites and start working on them. From websites such as `https://www.shadertoy.com/` or `www.glslsandbox.com`, and so on, you will get a simple text file with the extension, `.fsh`. Then you just have to add that shader code wherever you require.

Now, let's discuss about initialization and creation of new shader objects in our game.

The creation and initialization of new shader objects

The methods are discussed as follows:

- `Init! (name: string)`: This method initializes a new shader object by utilizing a fragment shader from a file present in the `app` bundle with a `.fsh` file extension. You pass the name of the file as a parameter and get a newly initialized shader object as the return value.

- `Init (source: String!, uniforms: [AnyObject]!)`: This method also initializes a new shader object using the specified source. But along with that, we can also set a list of `uniforms` to be added to the shader object. Uniforms are the way to access the data in fragment shaders. Uniforms have the same value for each pixel, for example, the size of the resulting image. We get an initialized shader object with this initializer.

- `Init (source: string!)`: This method initializes a new shader object with the `string` that contains the initial `source` for the shader object.

Let's discuss about properties and methods which can be used for uniform data with shader objects.

Uniform data in shaders

The methods are detailed as follows:

- `addUniform(uniform: SKUniform)`: This method adds a `uniform` object to the shader object. It takes the `uniform` object to be added as its parameter.

- `removeUniformNamed(name: String)`: This method removes a `uniform` object from the shader object.

- `uniformNamed(name: String)`: This method returns the `uniform` object resembling a particular `uniform` variable. If the `uniform` object is not found, it returns `nil`.

- `var uniforms: [AnyObject]`: This property has a list of all `uniforms` correlating with the shader.

To hold uniform data for a custom OpenGL SL shader, we use the `SKUniform` object. The uniform data is usable for all shaders that include the `uniform`.

Implementing shaders in the Platformer game

Let's implement shaders in our *Platformer* game and understand the integration of shaders much more closely.

1. Let's create a new `SKScene` in our game and load shaders there. We can have a button on the menu scene, which can take us to this scene.

2. Now add a new `swift` file with the name, `ShaderDemo.swift`, into our project.

3. Create a `SKSpriteKit` node with the name ,box, and import an image, `box.png`, of size 300 x 300 px. The box can be of any color but should only have one single color in it with no design of any kind. We are using this box image to add the shader effect inside the boundaries of the box. Also, set the position of the box image within the `didMoveToView()` method of `ShaderDemo.swift`:

```
let box = SKSpriteNode(imageNamed: "box")
 let location = CGPoint(x: CGRectGetMidX(self.frame), y:
CGRectGetMidY(self.frame))
  box.position = location
    self.addChild(box)
```

4. Next, we have to create the actual shader program, create a new empty file with the name, `blurShader.fsh`. We can get the code for this shader from any online resource. The following code has been fetched from `www.shadertoy.com`. Thanks to the Shadertoy team and its contributors for such a concise resource for us all. The `blurShade.fsh` file should look like the following code:

```
void main() {
#define iterations 256

    vec2 position = v_tex_coord; // gets the location of
    the current pixel in the intervals [0..1] [0..1]
```

```
vec3 color = vec3(0.0,0.0,0.0); // initialize color to
black

vec2 z = position; // z.x is the real component z.y is
the imaginary component


// Rescale the position to the intervals [-2,1] [-1,1]
z *= vec2(3.0,2.0);
z -= vec2(2.0,1.0);

//vec2 c = z;
vec2 c = vec2(-0.7 + cos(u_time) / 3.0,0.4 +
sin(u_time) / 3.0);

float it = 0.0; // Keep track of what iteration we
reached
for (int i = 0;i < iterations; ++i) {

    z = vec2(z.x * z.x - z.y * z.y, 2.0 * z.x * z.y);
    z += c;

    if (dot(z,z) > 4.0) { // dot(z,z) == length(z) ^ 2
    only faster to compute
        break;
    }

    it += 1.0;
}
if (it < float(iterations)) {
    color.x = sin(it / 3.0);
    color.y = cos(it / 6.0);
    color.z = cos(it / 12.0 + 3.14 / 4.0);
}

gl_FragColor = vec4(color,1.0);
}
```

5. Now, we just need to create the SKShader object with the pattern. Give blurshade.fsh as a file name and add it to the sprite node in the didMoveToView() method:

```
let pattern = SKShader(fileNamed: "blurShade.fsh")
box.shader = pattern
```

6. As `ShaderDemo.fsh` is ready to run, let's also add a BACK button in the shader scene for the user to go back to the previous screen. `ShaderDemo. swift` should look like the following:

```
class ShaderDemo : SKScene
{
    var menuSceneInstance : MenuScene?
    override func didMoveToView(view: SKView)
    {
        let box = SKSpriteNode(imageNamed: "box")
        let pattern = SKShader(fileNamed: "blurShade.fsh")
        let location = CGPoint(x:
CGRectGetMidX(self.frame), y: CGRectGetMidY(self.frame))
        box.position = location
        box.shader = pattern
        self.addChild(box)
        addBackLabel()
    }
    override func touchesBegan(touches: NSSet, withEvent
event: UIEvent)
    {
        for touch: AnyObject in touches {
            let location = touch.locationInNode(self)
            let node = self.nodeAtPoint(location)
            gotoMenuScreen()
        }
    }
    func gotoMenuScreen()
    {
        let transitionEffect =
        SKTransition.flipVerticalWithDuration(2)
        menuSceneInstance = MenuScene(size: self.size ,
        playbutton: "Play", background: "BG")
        menuSceneInstance!.anchorPoint = CGPoint(x: 0.5, y:
        0.5)
        self.view?.presentScene(menuSceneInstance ,
        transition:transitionEffect)
    }
    func addBackLabel()
    {
        var backbutton = SKLabelNode(fontNamed: FontFile)
        backbutton.fontColor = UIColor.blueColor()
        backbutton.name = "BACK"
        backbutton.text = "BACK"
```

```
        backbutton.position =
        CGPointMake(CGRectGetMinX(self.frame) +
backbutton.frame.width/2 , CGRectGetMinY(self.frame))
        backbutton.zPosition = 3
        self.addChild(backbutton)
    }
}
```

The following image shows how the code shader effect will look:

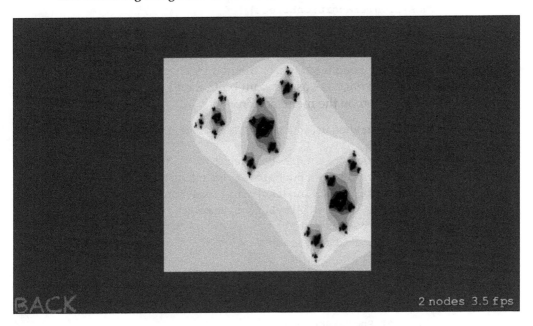

7. Let's also set up a button in `MenuScene.swift` for the user to go to the `ShaderDemo` scene. Following is the code for adding this button:

```
var shaderSceneInstance : ShaderDemo?
func addShaderSceneBtn()
    {
        var backbutton = SKLabelNode(fontNamed: FontFile)
        backbutton.fontColor = UIColor.blueColor()
        backbutton.name = "SHADOWS"
        backbutton.text = "SHADOW EFFECT"
        backbutton.position =
CGPointMake(CGRectGetMinX(self.frame) + backbutton.frame.width/2 ,
CGRectGetMinY(self.frame))
        backbutton.zPosition = 3
        self.addChild(backbutton)
    }
```

Now, the code is ready. For the sake of presentation, let's also add a transition for the button to present a shader scene when it is clicked:

```
func goToShaderScene(){
        let transitionEffect =
        SKTransition.flipHorizontalWithDuration(1.0)
        shaderSceneInstance = ShaderDemo(size: self.size)
        shaderSceneInstance!.anchorPoint = CGPoint(x: 0.5, y: 0.5)
        self.view?.presentScene(shaderSceneInstance ,
        transition:transitionEffect)


    }
```

Call this method from the `touchesBegan()` method by checking a condition if the node name equal to `"SHADOWS"` as we want both, the **PLAY** button and the **SHADOW EFFECT** button on the menu screen:

```
override func touchesBegan(touches: NSSet, withEvent event:
UIEvent) {
        for touch: AnyObject in touches {
            let location = touch.locationInNode(self)
            let node = self.nodeAtPoint(location)
            if node.name == PlayButton.name {
                goToGameScene()
                //goToShaderScene()


            }
            else if node.name == "SHADOWS"
            {
              goToShaderScene()
            }
        }
    }
    func goToShaderScene(){
        let transitionEffect =
        SKTransition.flipHorizontalWithDuration(1.0)
        shaderSceneInstance = ShaderDemo(size: self.size)
        shaderSceneInstance!.anchorPoint = CGPoint(x: 0.5, y: 0.5)
        self.view?.presentScene(shaderSceneInstance ,
        transition:transitionEffect)


    }
```

Now the file is ready to run as it should. The following screenshot shows how the main menu screen will look:

Summary

In this chapter, we learned about the particle effect and shaders in detail. We discussed about the `SKEmitterNode` object and the `SKShader` object, and how we can implement them in our *Platformer* game. We have also discussed about adding OpenGL ES code in our Sprite Kit project and how we can utilize shaders in our game. Now, our *Platformer* game has a particle effect when the player collides with the block, and the shader scene is a separate screen to display shader effects.

In the next chapter, we will add levels in our game, which will further enhance the gameplay experience for the user and help them understand the game concepts in more detail. We will also add a pause button that will pause the game when required.

8
Handling Multiple Scenes and Levels

In the previous chapter, we discussed a very significant topic of Sprite Kit, that is, particle effects and shaders. We also discussed about the `SKEmitterNode` object and the `SKShader` object. We also implemented them in our *Platformer* game. Implementation of shaders in our game was the most fun part.

In this chapter, we are going to discuss a very important aspect of a game, that is, the addition of multiple levels. Having various levels in a game makes the game more exciting as incrementing levels increases the complexity of the game, making it more difficult to play. As various levels are added to the game, it also becomes important to add a pause button, which will enable the game to pause whenever required.

Optimizing game levels

A game continuously running at the same difficulty will become monotonous, and soon the user will lose interest in it. So, how can you make your game interesting, exciting, and challenging? If your game keeps on increasing its difficulty and adds new challenges for the user, it will remain interesting till the end.

Different levels in a game are nothing but sections or parts of the game. Normally, in most of the games, the game scenes are divided into multiple levels. Levels divide a game into small excerpts and only one level is loaded at a time. In a game, levels can be denoted by different names, such as rounds, stages, chapters, acts, maps, worlds, and so on. Different levels can be represented via names or numbers. In case of representing a level by a numbering system, it is a clear analogy that the higher the number, the greater the level.

The names of the levels are the first impressions of a game's level; it is advisable to give a brief thought to this. Let's discuss about the naming of levels:

- **Utilitarian**: This mostly comprises of a number system or any other similar analogy. This system gives an idea to the player about their progress.

- **Location**: This requires using the location of the level as the level name, such as city, village, town, and so on. It gives an idea to the player about what he/she will be seeing.

- **Descriptive**: These seem more like being chapters of a book. This includes names such as airship fortress, green hill zone, pillar of autumn, and so on.

These are the three main ways in which you can name your game's level. Apart from this, one more method can be to have puny names for the levels. It all depends on you to name your level.

To complete a game level, the user has to pass through some constraints or difficulties, such as reaching a certain score point or performing a specific task to reach the next level. This is commonly known as game progression.

Programmers usually create different levels in one of the following two ways:

- **A new scene for a new level**: In this method, there is a new scene created for each new level.

- **Multiple levels in a single scene**: If the new level does not have much changes in the sprites or other game elements, we can also have the facility of multiple levels in a single scene. For the games which preferably have just one or two elements altered in each new level, single scene can be a good option.

A strategy for multiple levels

The different levels in the game define the difficulty of the game, or some hold the point at which the user currently should be, in the game.

In most games, level 1 will be the name of the first SKScene class for your first level. There are also a number of good transitions to choose from when transiting from one level to another or depicting any other effect, animation or information, as the level increases.

We can either use an array or a dictionary to store player data, such as items, health, levels achieved, and so on. Unless you have large amounts of data to be saved, NSUserDefaults can be the best option.

Core Data

For the larger data storage requirement of a game, we can use separate data files. For such types of requirements, Apple provides a powerful tool, that is, Core Data. This tool is very useful for storing level information, user information, and so on.

What is Core Data? It's a framework by Apple that acts as a bridge between your game and SQLite and other storage environments. Just like SQL, you can have tables, relationships, and queries. The advantages of Core Data over SQLite are that it requires no syntax and represents objects and classes unlike in a relational database.

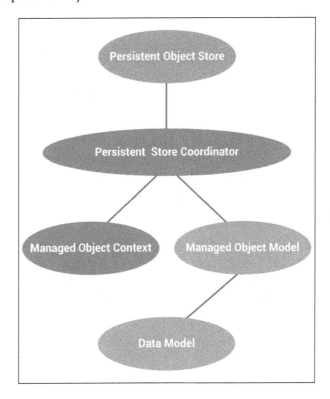

The important terms in Core Data are listed as follows:

- **Managed object model**: It is a tool that allows you to model classes (entities), relationships, and queries. (This is used by the Core Data framework.)

- **Managed objects [each row will be one object]**: This refers to the objects that are created in your game. These are your data classes, such as, player information, level information, and so on. Each managed object represents a row in your table (entity).

- **Managed object context**: This is an important object, since it manages all the relationships between the context objects that are defined in the model. It also keeps track of the status of the context objects. All interactions with the underlying database are done through context. The managed object context requests the persistent coordinator for data and tells it to save data when necessary.

- **Persistent store coordinator**: Through the persistent store coordinator, we provide a location on the device for data storage.

- **Persistent object store**: This is a data storage environment on the device.

Adding levels in our Platformer game

Let's add levels in our *Platformer* game. We are going to add the levels in a single scene. For the change in difficulty of the level, we can increase the speed of the player that is running and we can specify a distance after which the level will be increased.

Now, before we dive into adding levels in the game, first of all, we should know the current level being played. Hence, we are going to add the **Level** label in the game scene, so that the user can know about the current level being played.

Adding the Level label

The **Level** label is a simple text that will be displayed on the game scene and will act as a bit of information to recognize the level which is being played. As discussed earlier, you can have the name of the level as a number, location, or description. A number, as a level identifier, is the most common etymology in games. In our *Platformer* game, we are using numbers as level labels.

Add the following code in the `GameScene.swift` file. This code will add the `level` label functionality in our game:

```
func addLevelLabel()
    {
        self.levelLabel.text = "Level: 1"
        self.levelLabel.fontSize = 30
        self.levelLabel.zPosition = 3
        self.levelLabel.position =
CGPointMake(CGRectGetMidX(self.frame) + scoreText.frame.width ,
CGRectGetMidY(self.frame) + levelLabel.frame.height * 4.2)
        self.addChild(self.levelLabel)
    }
```

```
// ADDING LEVELS
    let levelLabel = SKLabelNode(fontNamed: "Chalkduster")
    var level = 1
addLevelLabel()
```

In the preceding code, we are adding the `level` label using `SKLabelNode` and applying the font, `chalkduster`. The initial level is set to `1` and from there, it progresses.

This is how the game will look after adding the `label` to identify the **Level: l**:

Adding levels

As the game progresses, the difficulty level increases. Increase of the difficulty level can be done based on any number of factors; we can increment the level when a player crosses a specific number of blocks, or when the score reaches a certain limit, or when the time increases.

In our *Platformer* game, we are going to increase difficulty levels based on the number of blocks crossed. As a game progresses, we are going to identify the need for a next level as shown as follows:

- **Level 1**: This level loads up at the start of the game
- **Level 2**: When the player jumps from the fifth block, we are going to start the second level

- **Level 3**: When the player jumps from the tenth block, we are going to start the third level

- **Last level**: When the player has jumped from 20 blocks, we are going to introduce the last level of the *Platformer* game

With every increase in level, we will also increase the difficulty of the game. In our game, we are going to increase ground speed, which will make the game more difficult to play.

The functionality to add levels is to be added in the `blockRunner` method in the `GameScene.swift` file. Following is the method with the functionality added:

```
func blockRunner()
    {
        // LOOP FOR THE DICTIONARY TO GET BLOCKS
        for(block, blockStatus) in self.blockStatuses
        {
            var thisBlock = self.childNodeWithName(block)!
            if blockStatus.shouldRunBlock()
            {
                blockStatus.timeGapForNextRun = random()
                blockStatus.currentInterval = 0
                blockStatus.isRunning = true
            }

            if blockStatus.isRunning
            {

                if thisBlock.position.x > blockMaxX        // IF IT
                IS POSITIVE (KEEP MOVING BLOCKS FROM RIGHT TO LEFT)
                {
                    thisBlock.position.x -=
                    CGFloat(self.groundSpeed)

                }
                else                                       // #1
                {
                    thisBlock.position.x = self.origBlockPositionX
                    blockStatus.isRunning = false
                    self.numberOfBlocksCrosssed += 1
                     self.levelLabel.text = "Level:
                     \(String(self.level))"
                    if self.numberOfBlocksCrosssed == 5
                    {
```

```
            self.level = level + 1
            self.groundSpeed = self.groundSpeed + 7
        }
        else if self.numberOfBlocksCrosssed == 10
        {
            self.level = level + 1
            self.groundSpeed = self.groundSpeed + 9
        }
        else if self.numberOfBlocksCrosssed == 20
        {
            self.level = level + 1
            self.groundSpeed = self.groundSpeed + 12
        }
        else if self.numberOfBlocksCrosssed > 20
        {
            println("Final Level")
        }
    }
        }
    else
    {
        blockStatus.currentInterval++
    }

        }

    }
```

In the preceding code, inside the `else` statement marked #1, the code to increase the level is added. The code has a nested `if`, `else if` condition where we have checked the number of blocks crossed, and based on that, we have increased the level and the ground speed of the game.

There are four statements in the preceding code depicting the level and ground speed increase. The second level starts once the player crosses 5 blocks, and the ground speed also increases. Similarly, the level and ground speed increases after 10 and 20 blocks.

Now, we have successfully added the functionality to increase the level once a certain number of blocks are crossed.

Following is how the **Level: 2** label will look when the player crosses five blocks:

For games with a higher number of levels, it is advisable to make a separate file for the level logic code. For example, if we had 10 different levels in our game, then we too would have created a separate file.

Adding the pause functionality

To pause a game during gameplay is an important functionality. Our game will benefit from the pause functionality; it will allow the player to continue from where they left off previously.

Let's add the pause functionality:

1. Primarily, we'll create a **Play/Pause** button for GameScene and configure the position and image for the button. We will add the following lines of code inside the GameScene.swift class:

    ```
    var pauseBtn:SKSpriteNode = SKSpriteNode(imageNamed:
    "PLAY-PAUSE")
    ```

2. Set the attributes of the `pauseBtn` label, such as `size`, `position`, and so on, as we did earlier for the other labels in the `addPlayPauseButton()` method. This is how it will look:

```
func addPlayPauseButton()
    {
        //self.runAction(sound)
        self.pauseBtn.name = "PAUSE"
        self.pauseBtn.zPosition = 3
        self.pauseBtn.position =
        CGPointMake(CGRectGetMaxX(self.frame) -
pauseBtn.frame.width/2 , CGRectGetMaxY(self.frame) -
pauseBtn.frame.height/2)
        self.addChild(pauseBtn)


    }
```

Please make sure that you call it from the `didMoveToView()` method also.

3. Now, we have to add the functionality to actually pause the game. We do this by adding the following code in the `touchesBegan()` method:

```
if self.pauseBtn.containsPoint(location)
        {
            if(self.view?.paused == false)
            {
                println("Game Scene is Paused")
                self.view?.paused = true

            }
            else
            {
                println("Game Scene is Resumed")
                self.view?.paused = false
            }
        }
```

The preceding code will pause the game when the button is pressed, and if the button is pressed again, the game will be resumed.

The following screenshot shows how the game will look after adding the pause functionality; a pause button appears in the top right corner of the screenshot:

Notice the pause button in the top right corner; tapping this button will pause the game.

Adding the NODE MENU button

We have created a node menu scene that displays examples of the nodes in a game. We are now going to add a button on the main menu, which will allow users to access the node menu scene:

1. Firstly, we have to create an instance of NodeMenuScene in the beginning with the following line of code:

    ```
    var nodeMenuSceneInstance : NodeMenuScene?
    ```

2. Now, we have to set attributes of the **NODE MENU** button label, as we did for the **Level:** label earlier. For this, add the following code in the addNodeMenuSceneBtn() method and call it from the didMoveToView() method also:

    ```
    func addNodeMenuSceneBtn()
        {
            var backbutton = SKLabelNode(fontNamed:
            "Chalkduster")
    ```

```
        backbutton.fontColor = UIColor.cyanColor()
        backbutton.name = "NODEMENU"
        backbutton.text = "NODE MENU"
        backbutton.position =
        CGPointMake(CGRectGetMaxX(self.frame) -
backbutton.frame.width/2 , CGRectGetMaxY(self.frame) -
backbutton.frame.width/8)
        backbutton.zPosition = 3
        self.addChild(backbutton)
    }
```

3. Now, add the following code in the `touchesBegan()` method to move for the node menu scene with a tap of the NODEMENU button we have just created:

```
else if node.name == "NODEMENU"
        {
            goToNodeMenuScene()


        }
```

4. Create a transition from our present scene using the following code:

```
func goToNodeMenuScene()
    {
        let transitionEffect =
        SKTransition.flipHorizontalWithDuration(1.0)
        nodeMenuSceneInstance = NodeMenuScene(size:
        self.size)
        nodeMenuSceneInstance!.anchorPoint = CGPoint(x: 0.5,
        y: 0.5)
        self.view?.presentScene(nodeMenuSceneInstance ,
        transition:transitionEffect)
    }
```

In the preceding code, we created the method, `goToNodeMenuScene()`, and added a transition effect for the scene to go from one to another with the effect of flipping horizontally.

The following screenshot shows how the main menu will look, after the button to the access node menu scene is created:

When someone taps on the button, **NODE MENU**, the node menu scene will open on the screen.

Summary

In this chapter, we added difficulty levels in our *Platformer* game. We updated our game by creating a level label and level increment functionality. An important feature, *PAUSE*, is now provided. Also, we learned how to add a scene in our game by integrating node menu scene through the **NODE MENU** button.

In the next chapter, we are going to discuss about performance enhancement techniques, along with some important extras that are going to be added in our *Platformer* game.

Performance Enhancement and Extras

9

In the previous chapter, we discussed about adding multiple levels in our game; adding multiple levels in a game is a normal functionality in most games. We also added the functionality to show the current level of the game by using a level label. Apart from this, we added a pause button and the button to access the node menu scene from the main menu.

This chapter is one of the most essential chapters in this book; here we are going to discuss about performance enhancement tips and tricks. Apart from this, we are going to add some really important features in our game. These features are:

- The scoring system
- The sound
- The running animation of the player

Sound is an essential part of a game; it greatly enhances the overall gameplay experience for the player. The scoring system helps the player to measure his or her performance over time. Running texture produces a good animation effect in the game, which increases the gameplay experience a lot. We are going to add all of these features in this current chapter, along with discussing about some of the important performance enhancement techniques for a Sprite Kit game.

Performance enhancement

Running a game requires extensive usage of memory and other resources of the device. This leads to accelerated drainage of the battery. We need to optimize the usage of the device resources for games. A game requires higher frames per second, hence more battery drainage occurs due to the excessive usage of the device resources. An optimized game will lead to efficient use of the device resources, hence less battery drainage. Following are listed some of the best practices to optimize the efficiency of a game:

- Systemizing a game's content in the scene
- Improving the drawing performance
- Improving performance with SKAction and constraints
- Improving the physics performance
- Improving the shapes performance
- Improving the effects performance
- Improving the lighting

Now we are going to discuss each of the previously listed methods in detail.

Systemizing a game's content in the scene

As we know, scenes are the elementary building blocks in a Sprite Kit game. A game can contain multiple scenes according to the requirements. A scene can contain multiple nodes, where the nodes can perform particular actions. We have a clear idea of how to create scenes, nodes, and actions for nodes. The challenging task is designing the game's scene and transition in such a way that it should not lower the game's performance.

One thing that should be kept in mind is that the scenes do not have a default behavior, as the storyboards do in traditional iOS app. Instead, we define and implement the behaviors for respective scenes, which may include the following:

- When to create new scenes
- Defining the content of the scene
- Defining when the transitions between the scenes should occur
- Defining the visual effect for transition
- Defining how the data is transferred from one scene to another

Performance enhancement by preloading textures

This is one of the most powerful ways of increasing the performance of a game. Sprite Kit provides two methods for the same:

- `func preloadWithCompletionHandler(completionHandler: () -> Void)`: This method uses a function that is responsible for loading the atlas textures into memory, which requires the parameter, `completionHandler`, which is called after the task is completed.

- `func preloadTextureAtlases(textureAtlases: [AnyObject]!,`

- `withCompletionHandler completionHandler: (() -> Void)!)`: This method loads the textures of multiple atlases into memory and calls a completion handler after the task is completed. The completion handler expects two parameters: one is `textureAtlases`, which is an array of the `SKTextureAtlas` objects, and the second parameter is `completionHandler`, which is a block called after the texture atlases are loaded.

Using texture atlases will reduce draw call, subsequently reducing the usage of the device resources. As of now, we have discussed some of the important techniques of performance enhancement in a game. Now, it is time to discuss about some essential elements of the game, such as scoring system, sounds, and so on.

Improving the drawing performance

The biggest part of building a node tree is organizing the graphical content that needs to be drawn. We should take care of what needs to drawn first and what should be drawn in the end. There are two factors which influence the drawing performance:

- Drawing order, by which the graphics are submitted to the engine
- Sharing of resources to accomplish the drawing

With respect to drawing order, you can set the sibling order of the node tree to reduce the number of drawings submitted by ignoring the sibling order:

```
View.ignoreSiblingOrder = true
```

You can use depth order as the rule to batch them together, and texture maps to optimize the batching further.

Make sure to turn on the performance metrics, such as **frames per second (FPS)**, node count, draw count, and quad count. These metrics will help you determine the performance of a game. Following are the codes that we can use to view the performance metrics:

```
View.showsFPS = true           // #1

View.showsNodeCount = true     //#2

View.showsDrawCount = true     //#3

View.showsQuadCount = true     //#4
```

In reference to the preceding code block, let's discuss each of the metrics:

- In code #1, we are displaying the number of frames per second in the game scene. The optimum FPS for a game is 60. By displaying the FPS in the game, it becomes easy to measure the FPS.

- In code #2, we are displaying the number of SKNodes in a scene. The lesser nodes we have in a scene, the better it performs. A game needs to have nodes in order to have elements in the game, but we can measure the FPS and nodes together to make sure how many nodes are producing the optimum FPS.

- In code #3, we are displaying the number of batches for the scene count, that is, how many batches the scene is going to draw. The lesser draws your game has, the better it performs.

- In code #4, we are displaying the quad count. Sprite Kit converts the node tree into rendered passes. Each of these rendering passes is rendered using quads. The lower the number of quads we have, the better the game performance.

Improving performance with SKActions and constraints

The main solution factor to increase the performance is by building the action once and using it for the maximum number of times possible. Try to avoid the custom animation code from the update() method. By using the SKAction and SKConstraint classes, you can optimize the animation effects in a game.

Improving the physics performance

Whenever SKScene computes a new frame of animation, it simulates the effects of forces and collisions on physics bodies connected to the node tree. It computes a final position, orientation, and velocity for each physics body.

With respect to improving the performance of the game, the dynamic objects cost more than static objects, so if possible, we can set the following property, so that the performance will be increased gradually.

Some guidelines for this are:

- You should use collision masks to group objects for performance
- You can use force fields to replace game logic
- You should turn on field debug drawing, if needed

Before assigning a specified boundary to a physics body, you must consider the most efficient shape for your object. The shape of the boundary defines the number of calculations/operations required to be performed by the device, costing efficiency. The **Circle** is the cheapest, followed by the **Rectangle**, **Polygon**, **Compound**, and **Alpha Mask** bodies in the order of increasing cost of computation.

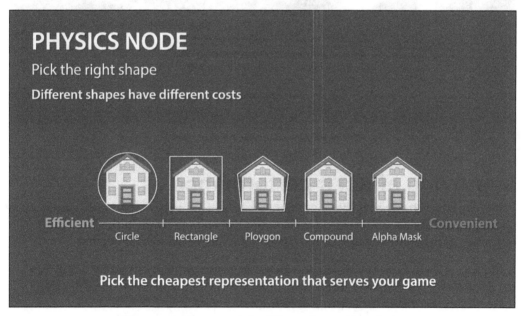

The computation cost scale for different shapes of boundaries

Improving shape's performance

The shape of an object node plays an important role with respect to game performance. Where the performance will be increased if the node requires a lesser number of computations.

In the same way as described in the physics performance topic, you can improve the efficiency cost of shape nodes. The polygon is the cheapest in terms of performance cost, followed by curves, linear stroke, stroked curve, and filled curve in the order of increasing costs of computation.

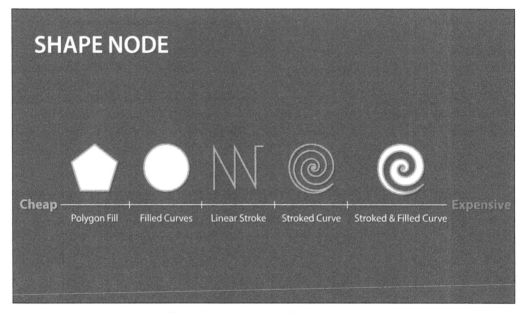

The performance cost scale for shape nodes

Improving effect's performance

With respect to effects in Sprite Kit, SKEffectNodes are expensive, hence, use it sparingly. It does its rendering off-screen and transfers to framebuffer, reducing efficiency. It is better to use SKShaders when no off-screen pass is needed.

If the effects do not change much, it is better to rasterize such effects by using the shouldRasterize property. If the shouldRasterize property is true, the effect node caches the image for use in future frames.

Improving lighting performance

Lighting is computed on a per pixel basis, hence the computation cost is proportional to the amount of pixels lit. Ambient light does not cost in terms of computation power. Computation cost of shadows is proportional to the number of lights, hence it is advised to keep the number of shadows low.

Measuring performance with instruments

Instruments is a performance measuring and testing tool provided by Apple in Xcode for the tracing and profiling of code. Instruments help in analyzing the performance of code. There are lot of instruments that can be used for checking performance issues, memory leaks, or other problems.

Once any issue gets identified, it becomes easy to rectify the issue. You can also see how much our game caches, and based on that, make a decision about the assets in the game.

You can access the instruments by navigating to **Xcode | Open Developer Tool | Instruments**. Then, you can choose the appropriate instrument to move with. It is better to have a look at the analysis in the initial phase of the development process, by this, you can easily understand which inclusion in the code was responsible for the error.

Instruments provide you with a list of trace templates. Trace templates are groups of preconfigured instruments. Let's discuss each of the trace templates in detail:

- **Activity Monitor**: The **Activity Monitor** is used to monitor the CPU, memory, disk, and network usage statistics processes.

- **Allocations**: The allocation tool is used to track a process's anonymous virtual memory and heap.

  This tool also provides the class names and optionally retained/released histories for objects.

- **Automation**: The automation template executes a script that simulates the UI interaction for an iOS application, which is launched from the instruments.

- **Cocoa Layout**: The **Cocoa Layout** observes the changes to the NSLayoutConstraint objects to help in determining when and where a layout constraint went away.

- **Core Animation**: The **Core Animation** instrument measures application graphics performance as well as CPU usage of a process, via time profiling.

- **Core Data**: This instrument template traces the **Core Data** filesystem activity, including fetches, cache misses, and saved caches too. This was discussed in *Chapter 8, Handling Multiple Scenes and Levels*.

- **Counters**: The **Counters** will collect the **performance monitor counter** (PMC) events, using time or event-based sampling methods.

- **Dispatch**: This template will monitor the dispatch queue activity, and record block invocations and their durations.

- **Energy Diagnostics**: This template will provide the diagnostics regarding energy usage as well as the basic ON/OFF state of major device components.

- **File Activity**: This will monitor the file and directory activity, including the file OPEN/CLOSE calls, file permission modifications, directory creation, file moves, and so on.

- **GPU Driver**: This template is used to measure the GPU driver statistics and it also samples active CPU usage.

- **Leaks**: The **Leaks** will measure the general memory usage; it periodically scans if an object is created and not accessed and detects the resulting memory loss.

- **Network**: The **Network** analyses, how your applications are using the TCP/IP and UDP/IP connections, using the connections instrument.

- **OpenGL ES Analysis**: This template measures and analyses openGL ES activity to detect openGL ES precision and performance problems. It also offers recommendations for addressing these problems.

- **Sudden Termination**: The **Sudden Termination** is used to analyze the sudden termination support of a target process, reporting back traces of file system accesses and sudden termination enabled/disabled calls.

- **System Trace**: This instrument provides system information such as process name, number of threads generated, CPU usage by each thread, and so on.

- **System Usage**: This template is used to record the I/O system activity related to files, sockets, and shared memory for a single process launched via instruments.

- **Time Profiler**: The **Time Profiler** is used to perform the low-overhead time-based sampling, where we can check the status of the processes that are running on the system CPUs. Profiling is a means of measuring, by which the output of a profiling session gives you an insight on what parts of your code are used most often, and tells you which part of the code can be improved.

- **Zombies**: If a game has removed an object, but at a later stage tries to access that object, it will crash the game. The Zombies instrument keeps removed objects as dead, and later on releases it whenever called by the game, hence, avoiding a crash. This way, the Zombies instrument points out where the game may crash. A debugger cannot pin-point this anomaly.

A scoring system in a game

Adding a scoring or points system in a game makes it more interesting and fun to play. Having a scoring system in the game makes it easier for the players to measure their performance, making the objective clear for the user.

It always makes sense to display the score somewhere on the main screen, so that the player can have a look at the score while playing the game.

Adding a scoring system in our Platformer game

In the first step of adding a scoring system in our game, we create a label node to display the score to the player. The initial variable will be zero.

Creating the Score label

Let's add the following code snippet in the beginning of the GameScene class:

```
let scoreText = SKLabelNode(fontNamed: "Chalkduster")
    var score = 0
```

In the preceding code, you are creating an SKLabelNode and assigning it to the font, Chalkduster. Along with this, you are also initializing a variable score with the value as zero.

Now, let's set the ScoreText label created above zero. Also, we can set the size and position of the font in an addScoreLabel() method and we can call this from didMoveToView() of GameScene:

```
func addScoreLabel()
    {
        self.scoreText.text = "Score: 0"
        self.scoreText.fontSize = 30
        self.scoreText.position =
CGPointMake(CGRectGetMinX(self.frame) + scoreText.frame.width /
1.8  , CGRectGetMidY(self.frame) + scoreText.frame.height * 4.2)
        self.addChild(self.scoreText)
    }
```

The preceding code will define the score text to **Score: 0** and the font size to 30. Along with this, we have also defined the position of the scoreText.

Following is how the game screen will look after implementing the **Score** label:

Incrementing the score when required

It is important to define when we have to increment the score in our game. The same should also be displayed in the scoreText label we have created.

As our *Platformer* game deals with blocks, which act as an obstacle, it is better to reward points to the player when he jumps over a block.

Add the following lines of code in the `blockrunner()` method with the condition that the blocks should successfully cross the player's *X* position without colliding with him (the first `else` condition):

```
self.score = score + 10

self.scoreText.text = "Score: \(String(self.score))"
```

Now, to save the highest score and the user's name, we will use a special facility provided by iOS to save frequently required data via `NSUserDefaults`, in the following way:

```
self.highestScore = self.score
NSUserDefaults.standardUserDefaults().setObject(highestScore,
forKey:"HighestScore")
NSUserDefaults.standardUserDefaults().setInteger(highestScore,
forKey:"SCORE")
```

The preceding code is to be added just before the end of the `if` statement, `blockStatus.isRunning`. The code will successfully increment score. Now, it is time to save the high score.

Saving the high score

We will add a popup screen to save the high score when the user scores a high score. To make this happen, firstly, we have to create a new scene, `ScoreList.swift`, and call this scene when the player is out, that is, when the game is over.

In our `didBeginContact()` method, we have the following code line:

```
self.player.runAction(SKAction.sequence(
[inOutActionWhenPlayerDied,
inOutActionWhenPlayerDied.reversedAction(),
upActionWhenPlayerDied,removeFromParent]),gotoMenuScreen)
```

Replace the preceding lines with the following ones:

```
self.player.runAction(SKAction.sequence(
[inOutActionWhenPlayerDied,
inOutActionWhenPlayerDied.reversedAction(),
upActionWhenPlayerDied,removeFromParent]),
completion: gotoSavePlayerScreen)
```

The new lines add the `ScoreList` scene when the player dies.

Now, we will create a new method called `gotoSavePlayerScreen()`, to check if the current score is greater than the saved score. Then, the `ScoreList` scene should be called, or else the main screen, that is, the `MainMenu` scene. The code for the same is as follows:

```
func gotoSavePlayerScreen()
    {
        self.player.removeFromParent()

        println("The Saved Score Is:  \(savedScore)")
        println("The Highest Score Is:  \(highestScore)")

        if self.highestScore > savedScore
        {
            let transitionEffect =
            SKTransition.doorsCloseHorizontalWithDuration(1.5)
            highScorerListInstance = ScoreList
    (size: self.size) // , playbutton: "Play", background: "BG")
            highScorerListInstance!.anchorPoint = CGPoint(x: 0.5,
            y: 0.5)
            self.view?.presentScene(highScorerListInstance ,
            transition:transitionEffect)
        }

        else if self.highestScore <= savedScore

        {
            gotoMenuScreen()
        }
    }
```

We have implemented the method to select the scene to open after game completion. Now, let's construct the `ScoreList` scene.

Creating the scene to save the high score

Let's create the `ScoreList` scene to display a popup for saving the highest score.

Also, add a label to congratulate the user. Following is the code for same:

```
func congratsUserAndSaveScorerName()
    {
        var congratsUserLabel = SKLabelNode(fontNamed:
        "Chalkduster")
        congratsUserLabel.fontColor = UIColor.redColor()
        congratsUserLabel.name = "CONGRATS"
```

```
        congratsUserLabel.color = UIColor.lightGrayColor()
        congratsUserLabel.text = "Congratulations!! "
        congratsUserLabel.position =
CGPointMake(CGRectGetMidX(self.frame), CGRectGetMidY(self.frame) +
congratsUserLabel.frame.height * 2)
        congratsUserLabel.zPosition = 3
        self.addChild(congratsUserLabel)
    }
```

We also need to add a **CANCEL** button if the user doesn't want to save the score with a name. Add the following code from the `didMoveToView()` method of `ScoreList.swift`, where the **CANCEL** button will take you to `MenuScene`:

```
func addCancelBtn()
    {
        var Cancelbutton = SKLabelNode(fontNamed: FontFile)
        Cancelbutton.fontColor = UIColor.blueColor()
        Cancelbutton.name = "CANCEL"
        Cancelbutton.text = "CANCEL"
        Cancelbutton.position =
CGPointMake(CGRectGetMinX(self.frame) +
Cancelbutton.frame.width/2 , CGRectGetMinY(self.frame))
        Cancelbutton.zPosition = 3
        self.addChild(Cancelbutton)
    }
func gotoMenuScreen()
    {
        self.playerNameTextField.removeFromSuperview()
        let transitionEffect =
        SKTransition.flipHorizontalWithDuration(1.0)
        menuSceneInstance = MenuScene(size: self.size ,
        playbutton: "Play", background: "BG")
        menuSceneInstance!.anchorPoint = CGPoint(x: 0.5, y: 0.5)
        self.view?.presentScene(menuSceneInstance ,
        transition:transitionEffect)

    }
```

The preceding code adds a cancel button in blue color, and tapping on this button takes the player to the MenuScene. Now, to handle the tapping on the **CANCEL** button, add the following code within touches loop, inside the touchesBegan() method of ScoreList.swift:

```
if node.name == "CANCEL"
{

    gotoMenuScreen()


}
```

The score list will have been successfully created. We have also added a cancel button for the convenience of the user. Now, it is time to add a textbox in which the player will add his/her name.

Adding a textbox to save player name

We need to display a textbox for the user to enter the player name that is to be saved. Add the following code line to insert a textfield inside a frame:

```
let playerNameTextField = UITextField(frame: CGRectMake(50, 150, 250, 50))
```

The following method will make the textbox that is to be used:

```
func addPlayerNameTextBox()
    {
        playerNameTextField.center = CGPointMake(self.size.width / 2, self.size.height / 2)
        playerNameTextField.backgroundColor = UIColor.whiteColor()
        playerNameTextField.placeholder = "Enter Your Name"
        playerNameTextField.borderStyle =
        UITextBorderStyle.RoundedRect
        self.view?.addSubview(playerNameTextField)
    }
```

Now, let's add a textFieldShouldReturn method of UITextFieldDelegate, to make the keypad disappear after tapping the return key while entering the player name in the textbox:

```
func textFieldShouldReturn(playerNameTextField: UITextField) -> Bool
    {
        println("Text Field Return Key")
        playerNameTextField.resignFirstResponder()
        return true

    }
```

Now, add the `UITextFieldDelegate` delegate to the `Scorelist` class at the beginning. This delegate enables the keyboard to appear.

The preceding snippet will successfully make the keyboard disappear once the return key is pressed. Now, the next task will be to save the added name.

This is how the screen will look when the keyboard is opened

Saving the player name with high score

We will name the button **ADD PLAYER**. This button will make the name entered by the user to get saved with the high score made. Firstly, create the following node, named add-player, with the image:

```
let addPlayerButton = SKSpriteNode(imageNamed:"add-player")
```

Add the following code method to set the properties of the **ADD PLAYER** button. Also, make sure to call the same from the `didmoveToView()` method:

```
func addScoresSceneBtn()
    {
        addPlayerButton.name = "SCORES"
        self.addPlayerButton.position =
CGPointMake(CGRectGetMidX(self.frame),CGRectGetMinY(self.frame)/3)
        self.addChild(self.addPlayerButton)
    }
declare the following variable before adding didMoveToView()
method

var highestScorerName:String = String()
```

Add the following lines of code in the `touchesBegan()` method of `ScoreList.swift`, as in the previous code, to handle the tap of the **ADD PLAYER** button within touches loop:

```
if node.name == "SCORES"
            {
                if playerNameTextField.text.isEmpty
                {
                    playerNameTextField.placeholder = "Please
                    Enter the Player Name"
                }
                else
                {
                    self.highestScorerName =
                    self.playerNameTextField.text
NSUserDefaults.standardUserDefaults().setObject(highestScorerName,
forKey:"HighestScorerName")
                    NSUserDefaults.standardUserDefaults().
synchronize()
                      gotoMenuScreen()
                }
            }
```

We are also adding `gotoMenuScene()` to return to the main menu as we know. Following is the code for it:

```
func gotoMenuScreen()
    {
        self.playerNameTextField.removeFromSuperview()
        let transitionEffect =
        SKTransition.flipHorizontalWithDuration(1.0)
        menuSceneInstance = MenuScene(size: self.size ,
        playbutton: "Play", background: "BG")
        menuSceneInstance!.anchorPoint = CGPoint(x: 0.5, y: 0.5)
self.view?.presentScene(menuSceneInstance ,
transition:transitionEffect)
    }
```

Now, the work on `SceneList.swift` is complete. Time to work on the high score board. The following screenshot shows how the screen will look:

Creating the high score board

So far, we have saved the name of the player who makes a high score, but we have not made a score board to show the high score to the player. It is better to have access to the score board right from the main menu, as it makes it convenient.

In our game, we are going to create a high score menu scene with a button on the main menu to reach this screen.

Firstly, create a scene with the name, `AddScoreScene.swift`, to show the high score.

Now, create the method, `showHeightestScorerName()`, to display the name of the player who scored the highest score, and also call the same from the `didMoveToView()` method in the `AddScoreScene.swift` file:

```
var savedScorerName: String = String()
func showHeighestScorerName()
    {
if(NSUserDefaults.standardUserDefaults().objectForKey
("HighestScorerName")) == (nil)
        { savedScorerName = " "
        }
```

```
        else
        { savedScorerName =
NSUserDefaults.standardUserDefaults().objectForKey
("HighestScorerName") as String
            println(savedScorerName)
        }
var highScorerNameLabel = SKLabelNode(fontNamed: "Chalkduster")
        highScorerNameLabel.fontColor = UIColor.blueColor()
        highScorerNameLabel.name = "HIGHESTSCORERNAME"
        highScorerNameLabel.color = UIColor.lightGrayColor()
        highScorerNameLabel.text = "High Scorer :
        \(savedScorerName)"
        highScorerNameLabel.position =
CGPointMake(CGRectGetMidX(self.frame), CGRectGetMidY(self.frame) +
(highScorerNameLabel.frame.height * 2))
        highScorerNameLabel.zPosition = 3
        self.addChild(highScorerNameLabel)
    }
```

We have displayed the name of the player with the highest score, now it is
time to show the highest score made by the player. For this, create the method,
showHeighestScores(), and also call the same from the didMoveToView()
method in the AddScoreScene.swift file. Following is the code to be added
in the showHeighestScores() method:

```
    func showHeighestScores()
    {
if(NSUserDefaults.standardUserDefaults().objectForKey
("HighestScore")) == (nil)
        {
            savedScore = 0
        }
        else
        {
            savedScore =
NSUserDefaults.standardUserDefaults().objectForKey("HighestScore")
as! Int
            println(savedScore)
        }

        var highScoreLabel = SKLabelNode(fontNamed: "Chalkduster")
        highScoreLabel.fontColor = UIColor.blueColor()
        highScoreLabel.name = "HIGHESTSCORE"
        highScoreLabel.color = UIColor.lightGrayColor()
```

```
        highScoreLabel.text = "The Score is: \(savedScore)"
        highScoreLabel.position =
  CGPointMake(CGRectGetMidX(self.frame), CGRectGetMidY(self.frame))
        highScoreLabel.zPosition = 3
        self.addChild(highScoreLabel)
    }
```

Now, it is time to add a back button, which will return the player to the main menu. Add the following code to implement the back button functionality:

```
func addBackBtn()
    {
        var mainMenubutton = SKLabelNode(fontNamed: FontFile)
        mainMenubutton.fontColor = UIColor.blueColor()
        mainMenubutton.name = "MAIN MENU"
        mainMenubutton.text = "MAIN MENU"
        mainMenubutton.position =
        CGPointMake(CGRectGetMinX(self.frame) +
        mainMenubutton.frame.width/2 , CGRectGetMinY(self.frame))
        mainMenubutton.zPosition = 3
        self.addChild(mainMenubutton)
    }


var menuSceneInstance : MenuScene?
 func goToMenuScene()
    {
        let transitionEffect =
        SKTransition.flipHorizontalWithDuration(1.0)
        menuSceneInstance = MenuScene(size: self.size ,
        playbutton: "Play", background: "BG")
        menuSceneInstance!.anchorPoint = CGPoint(x: 0.5, y: 0.5)
        self.view?.presentScene(menuSceneInstance ,
        transition:transitionEffect)
    }
```

The preceding code has added the back button functionality; now we have to handle the touch/tap on the button in the touchesBegan() method of AddScore.swift, as we did earlier. Add the following code in the touchesBegan() method:

```
for touch: AnyObject in touches
    {
        let location = touch.locationInNode(self)
        let node = self.nodeAtPoint(location)
        if node.name == "MAIN MENU"
        {
```

```
                goToMenuScene()
        }
    }
```

Following is how the high score board will look:

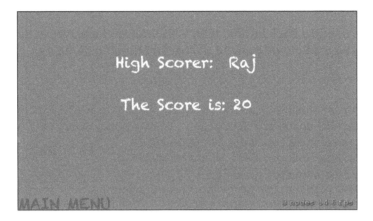

Finally, the high score screen is also complete. This concludes the integration of a scoring system in our *Platformer* game.

Adding sound into a game

A game can only be complete with different music and sound effects. There can be background music in the game along with sound effects at each action, such as, when the user taps, we can play a sound, and later, we can play a sound when a player hits an obstacle or some other element in the main game. We can also have different music at different levels. Sound effects play a vital role in enhancing the overall gaming experience, as they indulge the user in a holistic gaming experience.

Adding sounds into a Sprite Kit game

There are two ways to add sound effects in a Sprite Kit game:

- Using SKActions
- Using the AVFoundation framework

Adding sound effects using SKActions is not efficient, as compared to the AVFoundation framework. SKActions has a lot of limitations, such as that one cannot pause or play the sound in the middle of gameplay, and so on. Hence, it is advisable to use AVFoundation.

Adding sound into our Platformer game

Let's add sound effects in our *Platformer* game. We will be using the AVFoundation framework to add sounds.

1. Firstly, add the framework by clicking on your project, and then, under the **General** category, go to the **Linked frameworks and Libraries** section and add the AVFoundation framework.

2. Now, add the following code to import the AVFoundation framework into our GameScene.swift file:

```
Import AVFoundation
```

3. Add the AVAudioPlayerDelegate delegate to use specified properties and methods of AVAudioPlayer in the GameScene class.

4. Now, create an instance of AVAudioPlayer for our GameScene file:

```
var avPlayer:AVAudioPlayer!
```

5. We are adding two sound files named game_music.mp3 and Strong_Punch-Mike_Koenig-574430706.wav into our project (the WAV file format is suitable for short sounds, and MP3 format is suitable for longer durational sounds) and assign their names with two string variable as shown as follows:

```
let backgroundSound = "game_music"
    let gameOutSound = "Strong_Punch-Mike_Koenig-574430706"
```

6. Add the following method of code to make AVAudioPlayer get the specified audio file and play the same:

```
func readFileIntoAVPlayer(soundName:String, ext:String)
    {
        var error: NSError?
        let fileURL:NSURL =
        NSBundle.mainBundle().URLForResource(soundName,
        withExtension: ext)!

        // the player must be a field. Otherwise it will be
        released before playing starts.
        self.avPlayer = AVAudioPlayer(contentsOfURL:
        fileURL, error: &error)
        if avPlayer == nil
        {
            if let e = error {
                println(e.localizedDescription)
            }
        }
    }
```

```
    if avPlayer.playing
    {
        avPlayer.stop()
    }

    println("playing \(fileURL)")
    avPlayer.delegate = self
    avPlayer.prepareToPlay()
    avPlayer.volume = 1.0
    avPlayer.play()

}
```

In the preceding code, we are passing the sound name and the file format as two parameters. The method will then play the sound file. If the user, while playing sound on the device, starts the game, this code will stop the earlier playing sound and then start the game sound.

7. As we want the background sound to be always running, we will call the `readFileIntoAVPlayer()` method and pass `backgroundSound` and `mp3` as parameters. Add the method in the beginning of the `didMoveToView()` method of `GameScene.swift`. Following is the line to be added:

```
readFileIntoAVPlayer(backgroundSound, ext: "mp3")
```

The preceding line will play the background sound as the game starts.

8. We have also added another sound file for when the player dies. Now it is time to add the code that will play the sound effect when the player dies. Add the following lines of code in the beginning of the `didBeginContact()` method of `GameScene.swift`:

```
avPlayer.stop()

readFileIntoAVPlayer(gameOutSound, ext: "wav")
```

In the preceding code, we are stopping the background sound in the player and playing a new sound effect for the player's death by calling the same method as before, but with different parameters.

Animation frames using SKTexture

So far, we have used static images in our game, but if you will see, most of the games have animated effects, such as player running effect, car running effect, or any other effect that enhances the gameplay and creates a much better experience for all.

Adding the Run action texture to the player in the Platformer game

We had earlier added an image atlas of the name, idle.atlas, which contained similar images of the player standing position.

Now, we are going to add running texture images for the player, which will make it look as though the player is running in the GameScene.

Firstly, add a texture image set called bro5_run.atlas, which we have provided. The image atlas contains sets of seven images, which are sometimes also referred to as a sprite sheet. In our case, it will be known as the player running sprite sheet. These sets of images will be running one after the other at a fast rate of time inside texture atlas.

Now, let's assign the texture image for the player. Add the following line of code in the beginning of the didMoveToView() method:

```
player =
SKSpriteNode(texture:atlasForPlayerRun.textureNamed("bro5_run0001.
png"))
```

In the next step, we will add a method to create an SKAction for adding an animated texture for the different textures of atlasForPlayerRun.atlas. Add the following line of code by creating a runForwardTexture() method and call it from didMoveToView(). Make sure to do this after you have added the texture image for the player:

```
func runForwardTexture()
    {
        let hero_run_anim = SKAction.animateWithTextures([

            atlasForPlayerRun.textureNamed("bro5_run0002.png"),
            atlasForPlayerRun.textureNamed("bro5_run0002.png"),
            atlasForPlayerRun.textureNamed("bro5_run0003.png"),
            atlasForPlayerRun.textureNamed("bro5_run0004.png"),
            atlasForPlayerRun.textureNamed("bro5_run0005.png"),
            atlasForPlayerRun.textureNamed("bro5_run0006.png"),
```

```
        atlasForPlayerRun.textureNamed("bro5_run0007.png")
        ], timePerFrame: 0.06)

    let run = SKAction.repeatActionForever(hero_run_anim)

    player.runAction(run, withKey: "running")

}
```

The preceding code will have successfully implemented the running animation for the player. The following screenshot shows how a sprite sheet looks:

The texture atlas for a running animation of the player

Summary

In this chapter, we have covered some important aspects of the game, along with reading about performance improvements. Further, you can enhance the performance of your game using performance measuring instruments provided by Xcode. We also integrated the scoring system, sounds, and player running animation in our platformer game.

In the next and final chapter of this book, we will discuss each element of our *Platformer* game, take an in-depth look at the Game Center provided by Apple, and discuss the newest additions in iOS 9 brought to us by Apple.

10
Revisiting Our Game and More on iOS 9

Firstly, congratulations for overriding all the hurdles associated with the development of a game and making it to the last chapter. Now you are in a strong position to develop 2D games on your own, using the Sprite Kit game engine. In the previous chapter, we read about performance enhancements and added some extra functionality in our game, such as the scoring system, sounds, and player running animation.

In this chapter, we are going to finalize the game with a few final touches and discuss formidable bonus items that make your game super awesome. We will also read about integrating the game center to feed our game development experience to the fullest!

A recap on the development process of our Platformer game

Let's recall the whole development process of our *Platformer* game by discussing each of the scenes constructed, starting from the main menu:

- **Main menu screen**: This is the first screen we see, once we start the game. We have four buttons on this screen. In the top left corner, you will see the **SCORE MENU** button, which will take you to the high scoreboard. In the top right corner, there is a button called **NODE MENU**, which will take you to the node menu screen. In the bottom left corner, there is a button called **SHADOW EFFECT**, which will display the shadow effect. Lastly, in the centre of the screen, is the **PLAY** button. On tapping this button, you will enter the game screen.

- **Score menu screen**: This screen is the high scoreboard. You can see the high scorer's name and score on this screen. In the bottom left corner of the screen is the **MAIN MENU** button, which will take you back to the main menu.

- **Node menu screen**: This screen has various examples of nodes. You can see five different buttons called **SKCropNode**, **SKLightNode**, **SKEmitterNode**, **SKShapeNode**, and **SKVideoNode**. Along with these five buttons, there is a **BACK** button to take you back to the main menu screen. Each of the node buttons displays the respective example as the name of the button.

- **SKCropNode screen**: This screen shows an example of SKCropNode. You can see the cropping of a node in this screen. Along with this, there is the **BACK** button to go back to the node menu screen.

- **SKLightNode screen**: This screen shows an example of `SKLightNode`. You can see a light in the centre of the screen, which you can drag to see the changes in the shadow effect being created behind the images.

- **SKEmitterNode screen**: This screen presents an example of `SKEmitterNode`. You can see emitted particles on this screen, and along with this, you can also note the change in the number of nodes and **fps** on the screen, due to the regular creation or destruction of the emitted particles.

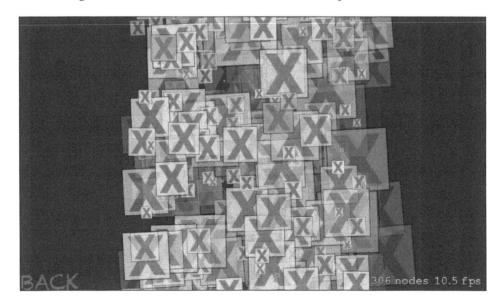

- **SKShapeNode screen**: This screen presents an example of `SKShapeNode`. You can see a shape in this screen, and as set before, by pressing the **BACK** button on the screen, you can go to the previous node menu screen.

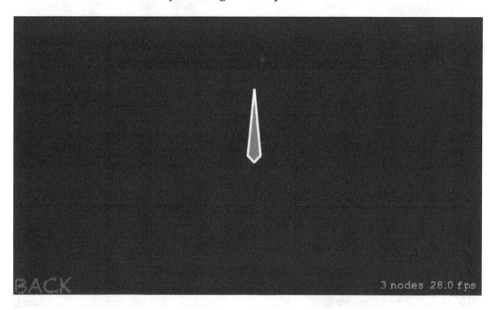

- **SKVideoNode screen**: This screen shows an example of **SKVideoNode**. You can see a video in the centre of the screen, and when you tap on the screen, it will start playing. You can press the **BACK** button to go to the previous screen.

- **Shadow effect screen**: This screen shows the shadow effect. You can view the shadow effect running in the middle of the screen, and like the emitter node screen, you can note that the **fps** of this screen is changing due to the shadow effect.

- **Game screen**: This is the game screen that has a **JUMP** and pause button. If the player hits any obstacle, the game terminates and the score list screen pops up.

- **Score list screen**: This screen is displayed just after the game is over. It has a **Congratulations** note and a textbox for entering the name of the player. Once you have added the name of the player, you can tap on the **ADD PLAYER** button to save the name of the player.

The preceding points briefly describe what each screen does and what elements are present on each screen.

Working further on the Platformer game

By now, we have worked on every essential aspect that is provided by Sprite Kit for game development. We have even integrated a scoring system, sound, and running animation to enhance the gaming experience. However, there is still room for further improvement; you can try out various effects and features, or just enhance the current features and make your game more exciting. Here are some ideas that you can, yourself, give a shot:

- **Obstacles**: Currently, we have only two types of obstacles; you can work on adding more obstacles in the game and make the gameplay a little more exciting.

- **Levels**: Currently, we have just three levels in the game, but you can work on adding more levels and make the game more challenging as the levels progress.

- **Extra life**: If the player hits an obstacle, the player dies; you can work on giving an extra life to the player, and hence, increase the gameplay time too.

- **Bonus points**: One more idea could be to add some bonus points when the player hits a special power-up. You can increase the score by an extra 100 or 200 points when the player hits this bonus item.

- **Sounds**: Our game currently has two sound effects: one is the background sound, and the other is the player's death sound. You can add more sounds in the game, such as different music for the menu and gameplay. Apart from this, you can have separate music in the node menu screen, and so on.

These ideas are just a beginning; you can apply a whole lot of creativity to the game and make it the next super hit title around.

An introduction to Game Center

Games on iOS and OS X platforms can utilize Apple's social gaming network called Game Center. Game players can compare scores on a leaderboard, track achievements, invite friends, or start a multiplayer game through auto-matching. The Game Center is a part of the Game Kit, which has two other functionalities apart from the Game Center.

The Game Center allows devices to connect to the Game Center service and exchange information. The Game Center also makes sure to add the information in the leaderboards and achievements. One can also play a multiplayer game using the Game Center service.

The advantages of Game Center in a game

The Game Center handles user authentication, friends, leaderboards, achievements, challenges, multiplayer, turn-based gaming, and invitations. In a way, it could be said that game center provides us with server services that are related to social interaction; something like its networking system. Some advantages of using the Game Center are:

- **No server side hassle**: With Game Center you don't have to worry about setting up your own servers. You can use the servers of Game Center for most of the tasks required in a social game.

- **User authentication**: Game Center also helps in authenticating the user, so you don't have to worry about duplicate IDs or any other such issues.

- **Friends**: You can play games with friends; players can interact with other players through an alias. Players can also set statuses, as well as mark other players with friends.

- **Multiplayer games**: You can play multiplayer games via the Game Center. Players can invite their friends or be connected to anonymous players across the Game Center network.

- **Turn-based gaming**: With this feature, you can have a turn-based network infrastructure. The match is played without all the players being connected to the Game Center simultaneously; the players play with each other via a turn-based method.

- **Leaderboards**: This allows the player to store the game scores at Game Center's scoreboard. Each of the games will have a local and a network leaderboard, where you can compare your score with local and global players.

- **Achievements**: Players can achieve various goals or accomplishments in a game and unlock achievements to gain special bonuses.

- **Challenges**: This allows players to challenge other players and compete with them for a score or an achievement.

Integrating Game Center in a game

Integrating Game Center in games is not hard, and on a macro level, consists of two steps:

1. One, is the implementation and integration of all of the Game Center's libraries that are required to be integrated in our game in Xcode.

2. The other step is to register the app on iTunes Connect, enable the Game Center support, and set up any leaderboard and achievements required in the game.

To integrate the Game Center in a Sprite Kit game, it is important to first have an Apple ID, so that you can register the game with Apple. Apart from having an Apple ID, it is also important to make some tweaks in the code and design to successfully incorporate the Game Center in your game. For example, you will have to do the sign-in (authentication) to the Game Center at game launch; if you wish to show leaderboards in the game, it is better to show them in the game itself, and so on.

Now, let's discuss both these steps in more detail.

Working with Xcode

You have to perform activities, such as the creation or integration of an Apple ID, for the game to be developed and to enable the Game Center in the Xcode. Let's have a look at the process:

1. To add an Apple ID, first click on the **Xcode** menu, **Preferences** in your Xcode. The **Preferences** windows will appear. At the top of the **Preferences** window, there will be various tabs. Click on the **Accounts** tab.

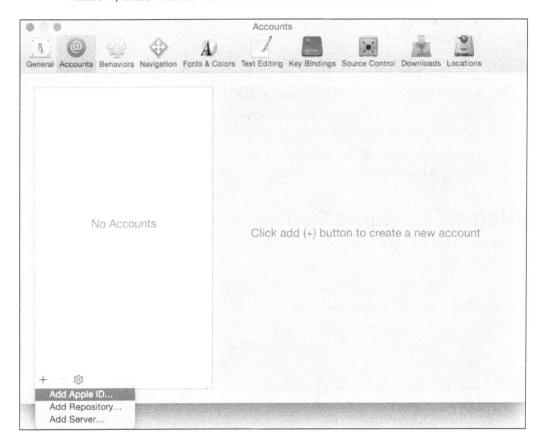

2. Now, go to the bottom left corner of the window and click on the button with the **+** symbol to get a small menu having three options.

3. Out of the three options in the small menu, click on the add **Apple ID** option. In the window that pops up, enter your **Apple ID** and **Password** and click on the **Add** button.

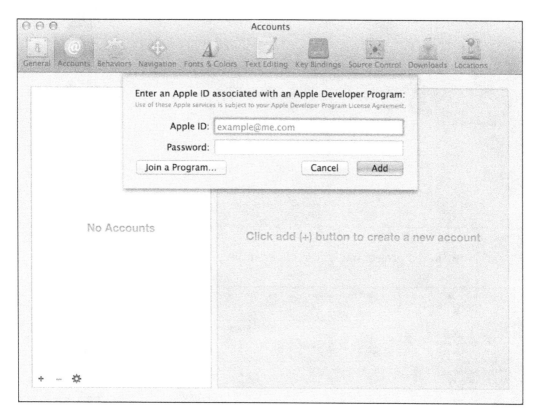

4. Now you will get a summary of your **Apple ID** in the **Accounts** tab.

5. Now, in the project navigator, click on the project target.

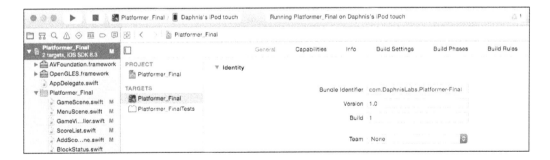

6. Under the **General** tab in the **Identity** section, there will be a drop-down menu named **Team**. If you click on it, you will see the developer's name inside it. It will confirm that the Apple ID has been successfully integrated. Then, you have to click on it to make Xcode use your developer account. Xcode to create the App ID automatically.

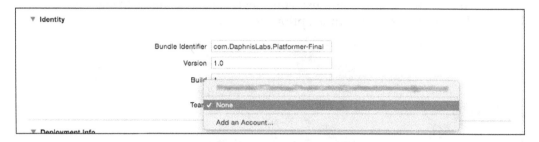

7. Now, click on the **Capabilities** tab that is just next to **General**. In the list of all the provided capabilities, expand the **Game Center** one. Now, turn on the switch on the right-hand side of the list.

The first step of Game Center integration in the game is complete. We have enabled the Game Center in the game and also created an App ID to be used by iTunes Connect in the next step.

Working with iTunes Connect

In this step, we are going to create a record in the iTunes Connect for a new application, and then we will manage the Game Center part by creating leaderboards and achievements.

1. Go to iTunes Connect and use your developer credentials to sign in. Then click on the **My Apps** option, among all the options.

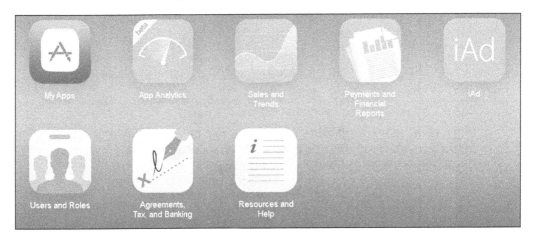

2. Then, on the upper right corner, there is a + button to add a new iOS app.

3. When you will click on the **New iOS App** button, you will get a popup window, asking for information regarding the new iOS app. The details asked are the **Company Name**, **Name** (app name), **Version**, **Primary Language**, **Bundle ID**, and **SKU**.

   ○ **Company Name** is the company's or developer's name (it cannot be changed later)

   ○ Next is the app name (**Name**), which cannot be longer than 255 characters

   ○ Next is the **Primary Language** in the app, which you can choose from a drop-down

- ○ The next option is the **Bundle ID**, which is a drop-down, and will be having a bundle ID of the app, present in Xcode
- ○ After that, you can add the **Version** number to be shown in the app store, and it should match the one used in Xcode
- ○ Finally, **SKU** is a unique ID for your app that is not visible on the app store

4. After you click on **Create** in the **New iOS App** popup, you will reach a page where you'll have to fill in details such as description, pricing, rating, and other release related options. From the tabs, there will be an option called **Game Center**. Click on that button to reach the **Enable Game Center** page.

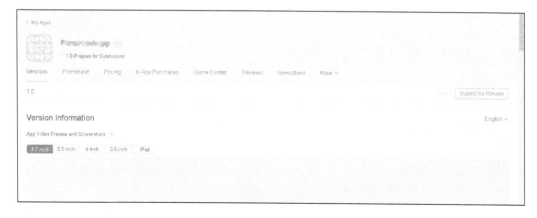

5. As you just have a single game, click on **Enable for Single Game**, and then, Game Center will become enabled for our game.

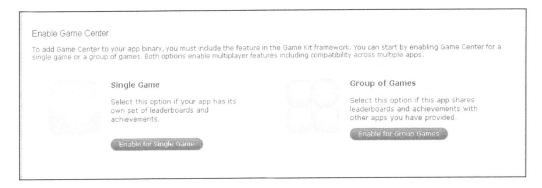

6. Under that, there will be an option to add the leaderboard and achievements; you can add them as per your convenience.

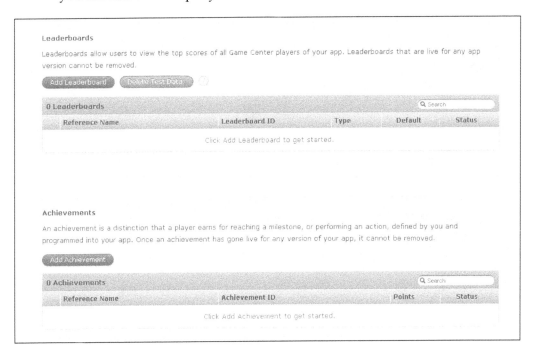

Now, we are through with the second step of the Game Center integration, which involves working with the iTunes Connect.

You have got a macro-level idea of what exactly has to be done to integrate the Game Center in a Sprite Kit game.

What's new in iOS 9

Apple announced iOS 9 in June 2015, and it will officially be released later this year. It is proposed to have some new features for the Sprite Kit framework. A few of them are mentioned in the following list:

- **Metal rendering support**: Metal provides lowest-overhead entry to the **Graphical Processing Unit (GPU)**. This enables us to maximize the graphics and computational abilities of our apps and games. Metal has streamlined APIs, multi-threading support, and precompiled shaders, which help make our game or app superior in performance and efficiency.

- **Improved scene editor and new action editor**: The latest version of Xcode now has a much improved scene editor and a new action editor. This will help in designing scenes in Xcode in less time with less code work.

- **Camera nodes**: Camera node is an `SKCameraNode` object and helps in specifying a position in the scene from which the scene can be rendered. If we set the scene's camera property to the camera node, then the scene is rendered using the camera node's property. This makes it even easier to create 2D scrolling games, belt scrolling games, and so on. The camera node in the scene determines which part of the scene's coordinate space should be visible in the view.

- **Positional audio**: We can add spatial audio effects with this feature. With this, the audio effects can track the position of the listener in a scene. An `SKAudioNode` object is used for the positional audio effect.

These features are a few of the important features launched by Apple for the Sprite Kit framework.

Summary

In this chapter, we discussed about our *Platformer* game and every aspect of it, starting from the first chapter of this book to the most recent one. We also discussed how you can apply new thoughts and ventures in this *Platformer* game and expand it further to make it the next big hit in the Apple app store. Lastly, we studied about Game Center and discussed in brief about its integration into a Sprite Kit game.

That being said, we are drawing the finishing line on our iOS game development book with the thought that a list of new games will storm the App Store, and this book will have been a great influence to the developers of those new platformer games. I am hoping to see some exciting titles from you guys. Good luck!

Index

Thank you for buying
iOS Game Development By Example

About Packt Publishing

Packt, pronounced 'packed', published its first book, *Mastering phpMyAdmin for Effective MySQL Management*, in April 2004, and subsequently continued to specialize in publishing highly focused books on specific technologies and solutions.

Our books and publications share the experiences of your fellow IT professionals in adapting and customizing today's systems, applications, and frameworks. Our solution-based books give you the knowledge and power to customize the software and technologies you're using to get the job done. Packt books are more specific and less general than the IT books you have seen in the past. Our unique business model allows us to bring you more focused information, giving you more of what you need to know, and less of what you don't.

Packt is a modern yet unique publishing company that focuses on producing quality, cutting-edge books for communities of developers, administrators, and newbies alike. For more information, please visit our website at www.packtpub.com.

About Packt Open Source

In 2010, Packt launched two new brands, Packt Open Source and Packt Enterprise, in order to continue its focus on specialization. This book is part of the Packt Open Source brand, home to books published on software built around open source licenses, and offering information to anybody from advanced developers to budding web designers. The Open Source brand also runs Packt's Open Source Royalty Scheme, by which Packt gives a royalty to each open source project about whose software a book is sold.

Writing for Packt

We welcome all inquiries from people who are interested in authoring. Book proposals should be sent to author@packtpub.com. If your book idea is still at an early stage and you would like to discuss it first before writing a formal book proposal, then please contact us; one of our commissioning editors will get in touch with you.

We're not just looking for published authors; if you have strong technical skills but no writing experience, our experienced editors can help you develop a writing career, or simply get some additional reward for your expertise.

Building Databases with Redis [Video]

ISBN: 978-1-78328-411-5   Duration: 03:13 hours

Acquire practical experience and skills in designing databases using Redis

Building Databases with Redis
Rostyslav Dzinko

1. Harness the power of the Redis to build storages as per your needs.

2. Execute Redis commands and discover ways to perform them on the database.

3. Filled with practical examples close to real-life tasks and situations.

Rapid Redis [Video]

ISBN: 978-1-78439-545-2   Duration: 00:49 hours

Get to grips with Redis; an open source, networked, in-memory, key-value data store that will solve all your storage needs

Rapid Redis
Scott Ganyo

1. Understand the difference between SQL and NoSQL databases.

2. Use Redis interactively through its command-line interface (CLI).

3. Understand the basic data structures of Redis and their usage.

Please check **www.PacktPub.com** for information on our titles

open source
community experience distilled

Building Scalable Apps
with Redis and Node.js

Develop customized, scalable web apps through the integration
of powerful Node.js frameworks

Joshua Johanan

Building Scalable Apps with Redis and Node.js

ISBN: 978-1-78398-448-0 Paperback: 316 pages

Develop customized, scalable web apps through the
integration of powerful Node.js frameworks

1. Design a simple application and turn it into the
   next Instagram.

2. Integrate utilities such as Redis, Socket.io, and
   Backbone to create Node.js web applications.

3. Learn to develop a complete web application
   right from the frontend to the backend in a
   streamlined manner.

Redis Applied
Design Patterns

Use Redis' features to enhance your software development
through a wide range of practical design patterns

Arun Chinnachamy

Redis Applied Design Patterns

ISBN: 978-1-78328-671-3 Paperback: 100 pages

Use Redis' features to enhance your software
development through a wide range of practical
design patterns

1. Explore and understand the design patterns
   of Redis through a wide array of practical
   use cases.

2. Learn about different data structures and the
   latest additions to Redis.

3. A practical guide packed with useful tips to
   help you use patterns in your application.

Please check **www.PacktPub.com** for information on our titles

www.ingramcontent.com/pod-product-compliance
Lightning Source LLC
Chambersburg PA
CBHW060555060326
40690CB00017B/3714